The Ultimate British Shorthair Guide

ERIC DE SOUZA

DISCLAIMER AND LEGAL NOTICE

While every attempt has been made to verify the information shared in this publication, neither shall the author nor publisher assume any responsibility for errors, omissions, nor contrary interpretation of the subject matter herein. Any perceived slight to any specific person(s) or organisation(s) are purely unintentional. You need to do your own due diligence to determine if the content of this product is correct for you.

This book is presented solely for educational and entertainment purposes. The author and publisher are not offering it as legal, medical, accounting, or other professional services advice. While best efforts have been used in preparing this book, the author and publisher make no representations or warranties of any kind and assume no liabilities of any kind with respect to the accuracy or completeness of the contents and specifically disclaim any implied warranties of merchantability or fitness of use for a particular purpose. Meither shall the author nor the publisher be held liable or responsible to any person or entity with respect to any loss or incidental or consequential damages caused, or alleged to have been caused, directly or indirectly, by the information or programs contained herein. The author shall not be liable for any loss incurred as a consequence of the use and application, direct or indirectly, of any information presented in this work. This publication is designed to provide information in regard to the subject matter covered. It is the reader's responsibility to find advice before putting anything written in this book into practice.

References are provided for informational purposes only and do not constitute endorsement of any websites or other sources. Readers should be aware that the websites listed in this book may change. We have no control over the nature, content, and availability of the websites listed in this book. The inclusion of any website links does not necessarily imply a recommendation or endorse the views expressed within them. The author takes no responsibility for, and will not be liable for, the website being temporarily unavailable or being removed from the internet. The information in this book is not intended to serve as legal or medical advice.

To all cat lovers.

CONTENTS

Introduction   **1**

The History Of The British Shorthair   **5**

Attributes Of The British Shorthair   **7**

Adopting A New British Shorthair Kitten   **15**

The Shopping List   **29**

Kitten Proofing Your Home   **33**

Helping Your Kitten Adjust To The New Life   **41**

Daily Diet   **51**

Dealing With Behavior Problems   **63**

Caring Guidelines For Your Cat   **69**

Finding A Vet, Medications, Vaccines And Other Essential Details   **79**

Breeding   **93**

The Importance Of Pet Insurance   **102**

Travelling With Your British Shorthair   **109**

Training Ground Rules For Your Cat   **121**

Showing Your Cat   **129**

Senior Moments   **133**

Cats And Babies   **139**

FAQs About Your Cat   **142**

Conclusion   **147**

INTRODUCTION

Welcome to the enchanting world of the British Shorthair, a beloved cat breed renowned for its striking appearance and gentle demeanor. This beautiful cat, with its dense coat and round, expressive eyes, has captured the hearts of cat lovers worldwide.

Originally bred in the United Kingdom as a working cat, the British Shorthair's sturdy build and adaptable nature make it a wonderful companion for families of all kinds. With its calm and affectionate personality, this breed is well-suited to life as an indoor pet, enjoying the company of its human family members and indulging in its favorite pastimes, from curling up for a nap to playing with toys.

In this book, we delve into the fascinating history and characteristics of the British Shorthair, exploring its origins, appearance, and temperament. We also provide practical tips for caring for this beloved breed, from grooming and feeding to training and socialization.

Whether you're a longtime fan of the British Shorthair or are considering adding one of these charming cats to your family, this book is the ultimate guide to all things feline. Join us as we celebrate the beauty and grace of the British Shorthair, a truly remarkable breed that has captured the hearts of cat lovers all over the world.

PART 1: ABOUT THE BREED

CHAPTER 1

The History Of The British Shorthair

To many people, the smiling British Shorthair is the epitome of a lazy feline who enjoys lounging around. The plump body of the British Shorthair is to blame for this misrepresentation. In reality, the British Shorthair is a farm cat developed in the 1880s from British farm, street and household cats, known for its skill in trapping and hunting mice and other small rodents. We'll go over all of this in great detail in the following chapters, but below you will find a quick rundown of this gorgeous pet.

Throughout history, The British Shorthair, which was created in the nineteenth century, became a very popular cat to own until the mid-twentieth century, when other unique breeds began to emerge. A group of dedicated cat lovers worked hard to ensure the survival of this beautiful, historical cat[1]. These wonderful cats were introduced in the United States until the late twentieth century. Cat fanciers became enthralled by their unusual personalities and size. This highly desirable group of pedigree cats can reach or even exceed 20 lbs./9.72 kg.

The British Shorthair comes in various colors. One, in particular, became so popular that it quickly became the only color recognized by cat associations for many years. The color of choice was called British Blue. Nonetheless, after WWII, this distinct color of British Shorthairs almost vanished. To preserve this beautiful shade of blue, cat lovers bred the remaining blue shorthairs with Blue Persians. This increased the gene pool and literally saved the specific shade from extinction. There are also orange-eyed or blue-eyed white, red or silver tabby, tortoiseshell, smoke, bi-colors, and point colors to choose from.

The sweet-natured British Shorthair has a circular-shaped head with broad cheeks and a short and thick tail. The British Shorthair, also known for its stockiness, is a large cat that normally weighs between nine and eighteen pounds. The British Shorthair, also known as the "four feet on the ground" cat is a companion that enjoys displays of affection. Although this breed is perfectly content to go about its business on its own it can also be socially inclined, making it suitable for those looking for friendly companions. We have also observed that while the British Shorthair can be truly content when his food bowl is full and has complete control over his activities, this self-contained cat does enjoy play and cuddle time.

This premium breed is not demanding and does not require much of an owner's time, it is an ideal addition to the family of someone who does not have a lot of free time at home. My cats, however, love meeting my wife and I by the front door every time we come home from an outing. With so many ancestors contributing to the gene pool, the British Shorthair is a very healthy breed overall. Another particular trait of this particular breed is that forty percent of all British Shorthairs have the rare type B blood. British Shorthairs are simple to care for and groom. Because their luxurious coat is dense and thick, a once-a-week combing session should be enough to remove loose hairs and dirt particles. Assume you don't have much time but still want a cat, or perhaps you have a family and your children want a pet. In that case, a British Shorthair's unassuming, self-contained, easy to care for and affectionate personality is definitely a worthy investment. It will undoubtedly be a perfect ailurophile companion whether you are single or have a family with children.

CHAPTER 2

ATTRIBUTES OF THE BRITISH SHORTHAIR

The British Shorthair cat exudes the British reserve, has a quiet voice, and is a low-maintenance adorable companion. While not overly affectionate, the British Shorthair gets along with everyone. They are calm and will tolerate other pets, and while they may not seek out snuggles at every opportunity, they are content to be picked up for a good cuddle. While some cats are known for being high-strung and jumpy, the British Shorthair is not one of them. If you're looking for a best friend who is as cool as a cucumber and won't bother you too much, this is the cat for you.

Coat Color And Features

The luxurious British Shorthair resembles a cuddly teddy bear with his short, thick plush coat, round head and cheeks, big round eyes, and rounded body. With a broad chest, strong legs with rounded paws and a thick tail with a rounded tip, his body is compact but powerful. The dense, crisp-feeling coat is available in almost any color or pattern you want, including lilac, chocolate, cinnamon, cream, fawn, golden, red, silver, black, white, pointed, tabby, tortoiseshell, long haired, shaded and bi-color patterns. Blue (gray) is the most common color, and the cats are sometimes referred to as British Blues. The British Shorhair has the most hair per square inch of any cat breed, with dense, plush short hair. Brushing your cat often will help remove loose hairs and dander while also preventing hairballs. These cats will shed their winter coats slightly more in the spring-autumn seasons, so you may need to brush them more frequently during this time. Visit our website muffinandpoppy.co.uk for brush recommendations and other top tips.

The well-mannered British Shorthair does not reach full physical maturity until he is between the ages of 4 and 5. The average British Shorthair size will be medium to large weighing normally between 7 and 18 pounds (3.2 and 8.16 kilograms) but sometimes more, with an average tail length of 12 inches (30 centimeters). With their round heads and chubby cheeks the British Shorthair seem to be permanently smiling out at the world. Lewis Carroll's choice of cat has been modelled on this breed for a good reason.

Temperament And Personality

The Cheshire Cat was, without a doubt, a British Shorthair. These affectionate, dignified cats enjoy attention, are normally quiet, but have bursts of crazed activity before returning to their affectionate, dignified self. They mature slowly, reaching full adulthood around 4-5 years of age, and get along well with dogs and other cats. They also tend to be tolerant and forgiving with children as long as they are not too rough as they do enjoy the attention.

British Shorthairs are laid-back, easygoing with a lovely nature. Males are large, easygoing lugs with a happy-go-lucky demeanor and a natural air of command. Females might take things more seriously and even display a posher poise. Both want to be with their people, not necessarily on their laps or carried around, but next to them or in the same room as them, ever observant, happily keeping all your secrets with rumbling purrs. When you are not present, they are content to entertain themselves until you return. This isn't a particularly active cat. You won't find him on top of the refrigerator but rather on the floor. He is intelligent and will appreciate having toys to play with, particularly if they are interactive.

Generally speaking, the British Shorthair is an easy going dignified cat. Strangers might be met with slight reserve, cautious curiosity or immediate happy interaction depending how your cat has been raised. Always keep in mind that every furball will have a unique personality and will meet new friends in their own way. The devoted British Shorthair may be shy with strangers until they warm up to them but that's because they are loyal to their cat parents and families. Saying that, you won't find these sweet-natured chubby cheeks experiencing any separation anxiety as they are perfectly content looking after the house for you, patiently waiting for your return just to meet you by the front door.

If your precious is on the overly cautious side just advise your guests not to give him attention and avoid eye contact. In cat language this is confrontational. If the cat decides to come and further investigate, keep energy levels calm and advise your visitors to slowly extend their hands so that the cat can smell them. This is how they say hello. Most cats will then start to rub up against humans, this shows that the cat is okay with your visitor. Only then a soft head or neck scratch might be allowed, it's never a good idea to invade their personal little spaces. It's also a good idea to allow your cat space to go off quietly to be by themselves and have some 'me time'. They never go far, however, so there is no need to worry. Toys and treats can also be used to encourage cautious cats to come out of their shell as they will associate people with yummy snacks or exciting things such as playtime. The British Shorthair is astute despite his laid-back temperament. They're clever and seem to have a sense of humour so have play time allocated and teach them tricks and provide them with puzzles and toys that reward them with treats when they learn how to manipulate them to keep their clever brain challenged and interested in life.

As you can see it's important to properly socialize your cat so they become familiar with human interaction. Teach them house rules and human integration when they are still young and they will not grow up to be overly fearful of new human friends but friendly and warm when new introductions are required.

Behaviour With Children

We live in a plug and play society but your cat is not a plug and play device. It is very important to allow time for them to get used to you, their new environment, children and any other pets you might have in your home. This could take from days to several weeks but it is worth it as you will gain the trust of a lifetime companion.

So, you have a new furry friend. How exciting! The question now is how do you get your new friend used to his new home? Here are three things to consider,

Safety. Perform a general risk assessment. Make sure that his new environment is cat safe. No poisonous plants, pieces of plastic or visible electric wire lying around.

Gentleness. Gently introduce your cat to the new environment. Give him the freedom to explore and sniff their new room, toys, litter, scratching post and new items. If they hide, sit quietly in the room and gently talk to them rather than forcing them out from their hiding spot. It is completely natural for cats to hide initially in a strange environment. Don't force any interaction in the beginning, and make sure everyone in the family is aware of this rule. Let them come to you.

Pace. For the first few days, limit them to just a couple of rooms to prevent them from feeling overwhelmed. As they become more confident, you can introduce them to other areas of 'their' new house. Once they feel confident with you, you can gradually introduce other members of the family. While it is easy to get excited, it is important to remember to introduce people at their pace – Although the British Shorthair is known for being very patient it can be overwhelming for your cat to meet everyone at the same time. Depending on their age children are bound to be loud and excited about the arrival of a new cat. Before your little ones meet their new friend, encourage them to be gentle and calm. It is important that the cat comes to them initially and they're shown how to gently interact with him. Use food as a reward to show the cat your approval. It is also worth noting that the British Shorthair is a large cat and usually prefers to keep their four paws on the ground rather than being picked up, so if your children want a nice cuddle let them do so under supervision. The British Shorthair breed does extremely well with children and if things are not to his liking, the ever patient Brit simply walks away rather than displaying aggression towards them. As your cat becomes more comfortable, He'll enjoy the playfulness of being around children. They love anything from paper balls to activity centres to elaborate scratching posts. Naturally, cats use their teeth and claws – making sure that your children play with your cat with appropriate toys instead of their hands and feet is important, particularly as their teeth and claws get bigger. Advise them to avoid using their fingers to encourage a cat in their direction too. In a nutshell you want to teach the cat that toys are for play and human hands and feet are not for them to pounce on. Children should also be made aware of the fact that if your cat is still young he will require a lot of sleep and will need to be left alone to rest, especially as he gets used to his new home. If you have a new baby in the home make the necessary sleeping arrangements before your baby arrives. Invest in simple netting to place over the cot if necessary. Let your cat smell the baby and try not to change your cat's routine and do not leave your baby and cat unattended until they are both mature enough.

Behaviour With Other Pets

The British Shorthair do well on their own but do not oppose other pets living in 'their' home. Although it's always best to introduce them to each other when they are young, after an initial huffing and puffing, the British Shorthair will get along with a dog or new cat just fine. Introductions should be made slowly and in a safe way by keeping the cat inside the pet carrier and the dog on a leash for example. Alternatively, restrict your dog (or new cat) to a new room and allow the resident cat full rein of the house as normal and allow the resident cat make the first move and never introduce a new pet to your cat by putting them nose to nose.

For smaller pets such as fish, hamsters or birds the best thing to do is to perform a risk assessment and limit opportunities for disaster and by not leaving them alone unattended. Remember that you're still dealing with a cat and they might be looking at the new fluffy (and smaller) creature as prey. British Shorthairs are not intentionally naughty or destructive cats but they do know how to problem solve and can jump and climb very well, so keep contact safely under close supervision or close off smaller animals from the cat's area.

Behaviour With The Outside Environment

British Shorthairs are perfectly content house cats and will not intentionally try to escape. Neutered or spayed cats are even less prone to doing so. Give them quality food, water, toys and a scratching post and they will be happy in 'their' homes. However, cats are natural athletes and can jump approximately five times their own height. They are adept climbers, can squeeze through cracks and will be superior at escaping confinement if necessary. As natural hunters they will not hesitate to chase butterflies or curious little birds that might venture near their immediate territory, which could mean falling from a window, crossing a busy road or being chased by a dog. The expensive British Shorthair is not a streetwise cat and will trust their outside environment a little too much resulting in early death or injury. The modern world tends to be a dangerous place for our beloved companions. Whether danger arises from vehicles, aggressive dogs, wildlife, parasites or mean humans, the risk is not worth it. I would never dream of allowing my cats access to the outside world. A suitable compromise would be a cat safe garden adaptation, chalets or a catio, a secure enclosed structure that allows cats to be contained while enjoying the sunlight and fresh air and the sounds of the outside world. My best advice is to not allow them outside unless a safe enclosed garden or suitable environment has been provided.

About Their Health

All cats, just like all people, have the potential to develop genetic health problems. Avoid breeders who claim that their breed has no health or genetic issues. They are either telling fibs or ignorant of the breed. Avoid breeders who do not provide at least four week free insurance, who claim that the breed is 100% healthy and has no known problems, or who claim that their kittens are separated from the rest of the household for health reasons.

In general, the British Shorthair is a very healthy cat. Although extremely rare, due to selective breeding, they still are predisposed to hip dysplasia, hypertrophic cardiomyopathy (HCM) and hemophilia B, a hereditary bleeding disorder. The most common type of heart disease in cats is hypertrophic cardiomyopathy (HCM). It causes the heart muscle to thicken (hypertrophy). An echocardiogram can determine whether or not a cat has HCM. Avoid breeders that claim to have HCM-free lines. Nobody can promise that their cats will never develop HCM. Responsible breeders will always stop breeding cats with HCM as they should be removed from breeding programs.

Hip Dysplasia is another rare condition defect in the hip socket. A cat affected by this problem will move very slowly and show a marked reluctance to jump or climb. The condition presents with a range of severities from mild and annoying to painful and debilitating. There is no way to guarantee that the defect will not show up in any cat breed. Keeping normal, healthy body weight is a critical component of managing hip dysplasia over a cat's lifetime. Medication may be required for pain control, and at times corrective surgery is necessary.

Remember that once you've adopted a new kitten, you can protect your precious friend from one of the most common health issues: obesity. One of the simplest ways to protect a British Shorthair's overall health is to keep him at a healthy weight. As a guide you should be able to feel your cat's ribs easily when you stroke their body lightly and you should clearly see a waistline when you look at them from above. If you like to give your cat treats, reduce the amount of normal food you provide. Use preventive measures, such as moderation and exercise, to help ensure a healthier cat for life.

Pros And Cons Of The Breed

This is largely due to perception and personal taste. I absolutely love the British Shorthair cat and have observed over the years that the joys of having them in my life far outweighs any argument against them.

Pros
- Luxurious and noble.
- Calm and sedate.
- Adapt well to most circumstances.
- Intelligent and loyal.
- Great house cats.
- Friendly and affectionate.
- Not prone to separation anxiety.
- Shed in moderation.
- Good with children and other pets.
- Generally quiet and not overly vocal like the Siamese breed.
- Do not tend to be destructive.
- Tend to be healthy, hardy cats.
- Medium to big cats at 7 - 18 lbs. / 3.2 - 8.16 kg.
- Live about 14-18 years on average, but 20 is also possible.

Cons
- Expensive
- Might not be a lap cat.
- Don't always like to be carried.

- Don't usually like to be held or restrained.
- Somewhat prone to obesity.
- Not jumpers but they will climb if they're curious about something.
- Initially shy around new people.
- Although they have few genetic problems, hip dysplasia and hypertrophic
- cardiomyopathy do appear in the breed.

CHAPTER 3

ADOPTING A NEW BRITISH SHORTHAIR KITTEN

Do your homework before bringing your British Shorthair home if you want him to be happy and healthy so you can enjoy your time with him. You might want to visit the Governing Council of the Cat Fancy (GCCF), The International Cat Association (TICA) and Cat Fanciers Association (CFA) for more information on the history, personality, and appearance of the British Shorthair, as well as to find breeders. Although cat parents often say that owning a British Shorthair is an investment, a decision to share your life with a new companion should never be entered into lightly.

It is always beneficial to ask yourself questions regarding,

Your living environment. Is my landlord okay with me having a cat? Have I performed an in-depth risk assessment? Is my house cat safe? Is my environment clean and healthy for my new companion? Do I need a grill or any other safety device for my windows? Is my house by a busy main road? Is my garden safe for my cat? Is there a chance that my cat may be attacked by my neighbour's dog? Do I have allergies? Do my children know how to handle cats? What is the number one reason why I want a cat in my life? Is there anything else that requires my attention?

Affordability. Have I considered my Budget? Do I need to make one? Can I afford my cat's monthly expenses? Registered kittens from established breeders sell for £1,000 - £3,00o / $1,300 - $4146.90, initial accessories (bowls, scratching posts, blanket) £20 - £150 / $27 - $54 depending on taste and how expensive they are, pet insurance approximately £10 / $13 monthly, quality food on average costs £40 - £80 / $54 - $108 .

Time. Have I spent enough time researching the breed? Hopefully this book will help you to do just that. Do I like to travel a lot? Do I have time and patience to devote to a cat? British Shorthairs are not demanding cats, however, if you want a healthy and happy friend you should not neglect spending time with them. Playtime, grooming, kind words of affirmation, stroking don't have to take all day but all form part of the human-cat bonding process. So, be prepared to reserve daily time to spend with your cat.

A reputable breeder will follow an ethics code that prohibits sales to pet stores and wholesalers and defines the breeder's responsibilities to their cats and buyers. Select a responsible breeder who raises kittens in their home. Isolated kittens can become fearful and skittish, making it difficult to socialize them later in life.

There are many reputable breeders with websites, so how do you know who is good and who is not? Kittens should always be available; there should be multiple litters on the premises. You should choose any kitten, and you should be able to pay online with a credit card or via bank transfer. These items are useful, but they are rarely associated with reputable breeders. Whether you plan to get your feline friend from a breeder, a pet store, or somewhere else, remember the old adage let the buyer beware. Disreputable breeders and unhealthy catteries can be difficult to distinguish from reputable businesses. There is no foolproof way to avoid buying a sick kitten, but researching the breed (so you know what to expect), inspecting the facility (identifying unhealthy conditions or sick animals), and asking the right questions can reduce the chances of ending up in a bad situation. Don't forget to ask your veterinarian, who can frequently refer you to a reputable breeder, breed rescue organization, or another dependable source for healthy kittens such as the GCCF (UK) or the CFA (USA) as you will see below. A reputable breeder will provide you with,

- [ ] a GCCF or TICA registration card.
- [ ] a vet card with two vet checks and vaccination visits at 9 and 12 weeks.
- [ ] a dewormed and deflead kitten.
- [ ] proof of microchipping.
- [ ] a litter trained kitten.
- [ ] a pedigree certificate.
- [ ] four weeks free insurance.
- [ ] a well groomed kitten.

Put in at least as much time and effort into researching your kitten as you would in selecting a new car or high-priced appliance. In the long run, it will save you money. And please be patient. Depending on what you're looking for, you could be looking for a kitten for six months or more. By the age of 12 weeks, the kittens will already have been weaned, litter and scratching post trained, received their basic inoculations and become bonded with humans.

Many breeders do not place kittens in new homes until they are between 12 and 13 weeks and are absolutely sure the new owners will spoil them rotten.

The GCCF, TICA, CFA websites are good places to start if you are looking for a pedigree cat. Google search can also be an alternative way to find a British Shorthair companion as long as you stick with reputable breeders by following the guidelines above. Also, consider whether an adult British Shorthair would be a better fit for your lifestyle before purchasing a kitten. Kittens are a lot of fun, but they're also a lot of work and can be slightly more destructive until they reach more mature adulthood. You know more about what you're getting with an adult in terms of personality and health. If you prefer an adult cat over a kitten, inquire with breeders about purchasing a retired show or breeding cat or if they know of an adult cat in need of a new home.

If at any point you feel that you can no longer look after your cat you must contact the breeder as they might have space available. You will have to have your cat thoroughly vet checked mainly for ringworm, FEL/FIV and parasites before returning it, but you will at least have a safe place to rehome your cat if necessary.

I strongly encourage you to consider the above points before you decide to share your life with a cat no matter how low maintenance they are. You will spend the next sixteen to twenty years of your life with a consistent friend that will enjoy being with you every moment you allow them to after all.

Choosing A Kitten

Kittens are highly trainable and British Shorthairs tend to be very similar in their temperament but generally speaking when choosing a kitten ask the breeder, or if you have the opportunity, look for the most friendly and outgoing one rather than an overly fearful or aggressive kitten. Look for a kitten that demonstrates good social skills with their siblings. Over the years I have observed that British Shorthairs tend to develop strong bonds with their humans. Our new additions still follow my daughter around the house as she was the main person in the house who mothered them. They absolutely love her to bits.

British Shorthairs are great friends of other pets, if you have other animals in the house again a very general guide would be to look for kittens that love playing with each other and don't mind being at the bottom or top when wrestling as that might indicate that they usually play well with others. Observe whether they share their toys and whether they like the company of the other kittens as opposed to trying to be all by themselves. Finally, most kittens just want to run around and play to their heart's content but you can also try to observe which kitten first comes to you or even don't mind being held for a couple of minutes. In addition, find out how the breeder works with the kittens to ensure they are well socialized. Some of the hallmarks of a solid socialization program include:

- ☐ Frequent handling and grooming.
- ☐ Exploration time.
- ☐ Interaction with other humans, cats and kittens.
- ☐ Intellectual stimulation through toys and games.
- ☐ If possible supervised exposure to dogs and children.
- ☐ Comfort level with reasonable noise.

Cats are not the self-sufficient loners some people usually make them out to be. They might do fine during the day but they will cherish a good dose of attention from you, even greeting you at the door to hear about your day.

Emotional health is important but how about physical health? Although your kitten should leave fully vet checked and ready, it's always a good idea to make an appointment with your own veterinarian. Before this stage, however, you can ask the breeder or cat shelter for this information or even perform a general health yourself by checking the following:

Breathing. This should be done quietly, without coughing or sneezing. The nostrils should be free from crusting or discharges.

Body. Their little tunny should look round and full.

Coat. Check for dandruff, bald spots or greasiness.

Genitals. Are there any discharges from the kitten's genitals or anal region?

Vision. Weepy eyes seem to occur in cats with flatter faces, but are the kitten's eyes red, crusty and with a non-clear type of discharge? Can they notice if you play with them using a string?

Hearing. Can the kitten react if you snap your finger behind his ear?

Mobility. Healthy kittens tend to be alert and energetic. Can they walk, jump and run without any wobbling or limping?

Don't be surprised if the kitten is a little shy at first. That's normal, and if you're asked to use a hand sanitizer or wear a disposable top first, don't be offended. Many diseases are so easily transmissible they can be passed from one animal to another with just a nose tap. Moreover, chances are the kittens are not fully vaccinated yet, so sanitising your hands or wearing provided disposable garments is for the protection of the kittens and not a reflection on you.

Adopting A Kitten From A Breeder

It's important to understand that visiting a cattery or dealing with a breeder is not a drive-thru. You may get turned down if a breeder thinks you are not a good candidate to raise one of their kittens. Expect to be required to sign a contract agreeing that the kitten you adopt will be spayed or neutered before it reaches 12 months of age and that you will provide proof of this. Some breeders will not release full pedigree papers until they receive this. You might be asked questions about your home life, your schedule, and your prior experience with cats and with the British Shorthair breed. This is not unreasonable, this is the breeder's job. They must put the welfare of the cats they raise first. If this is your first time as a car parent, say so. Breeders want to know that the kitten is going to a good home with loving and attentive 'parents'. Treating your breeder well and making friends with them gives you access to someone who knows the breed and can help you with your questions. This is an important relationship and one you want to nurture.

You might also have your own questions. Here are some pre-adoption questions you might ask the breeder. Be sure that you go over these points to your satisfaction.

Have the kitten's parents been healthy throughout their lives?

Can I meet and maybe interact with the kitten's parents? You should always be able to see the mother.

Has the kitten received any vaccinations, and if so, when are the booster shots to be administered?

Where do the kittens live? Although nice chalets are acceptable, it's always good for kittens to have experienced constant touch and household activity of life indoors. Saying that our eldest cat came from a reliable breeder, raised in a cattery and has the most friendly, sociable skills and love for a good lap than any of our other cats.

Will I receive copies of all of the kitten's records at the time of adoption?

Is there a kitten care manual for the kitten which includes food and litter type, guide to basic accessories and the kittens feeding routine?

Has the kitten seen a vet for any other reason? If so, why and what treatment was administered?

If necessary, ask for a complete summary of all veterinary care the kitten has received and copies of the complete records to pass on to your own veterinarian.

Adopting A Cat From A Shelter Or British Shorthair Rescue Centre

The British Shorthair is a rare breed. It's unlikely that you'll find one in a shelter or through a rescue organization. Pedigreed cats may end up at the shelter after losing their home due to an owner's death, divorce, or a change in economic circumstances. Check out the listings on Petfinder, Adopt-a-Pet.com, PetAdoptionUK or the Fanciers Breeder Referral List, and ask breeders if they know of any British Shorthairs that need a new home if you wish to go down that route. Wherever you get your British Shorthair, make sure you have a good contract with the shelter or rescue group that outlines both parties' responsibilities. If your state has pet lemon laws (the right to return), make sure you and the person from whom you purchased the cat are both aware of your rights and options.

You might also have questions. Here are some pre-adoption questions you might ask the shelter or rescue center.

Was it lost or handed in?

If handed in, why? This could indicate a behaviour issue.

Has any behaviour testing been carried out? If so, can I see the report?

Can you help with any future problems?

Take your British Shorthair, kitten or adult cat, to your veterinarian as soon as you can after adoption. Your veterinarian will be able to detect problems and work with you to develop a preventive regimen that will help you avoid various health problems.

Basic Needs

Grooming

You want your British Shorthair kitten to get used to a daily grooming routine as soon as possible to prevent them from getting traumatised every time grooming is needed.

The plush coat of the British Shorthair is easy to groom and shed in moderation, requiring only weekly combing or brushing to remove dead hair, distribute skin oils and to and keep it lush. Brush your cat more frequently in the spring and autumn, when they shed their coat in preparation for new growth. Comb the British Longhair daily to prevent or remove tangles and mats. An effective routine should include not just surface brushing, but also sensitive areas that are easily missed around the ears and collar area, the armpit area, the back end and tail.

The rest is routine care. Claw clipping is done as needed, usually once a week. Examine the ears once a week for redness or a bad odor, which could indicate an infection. If their ears appear dirty, use a cotton ball dampened with water or a gentle cleanser recommended by your veterinarian to clean them. Soft damp cloths can also be dipped in a 50-50 mixture of apple cider vinegar and warm water if necessary. Cotton swabs should be avoided because they can cause damage to the ear's interior.

You can also brush your pet's teeth regularly with a vet-approved pet toothpaste for good overall health and fresh breath. For the eyes use a soft, damp cloth to wipe the corners of the eyes to remove any discharge. To avoid the spread of infection, use a separate area of the cloth for each eye.

Last but not least, maintain a spotless litter box. Cats are extremely conscientious about bathroom hygiene.

Coat brushing, claw clipping, and teeth brushing should begin as soon as possible so that your kitten becomes accustomed to the activity. Your cat might not like or approve of their grooming regimen but it's absolutely necessary that your cat gets used to it as this will help them to be comfortable while being handled, prevent hairball and help them to bond with their human parent.

Another important point to note is that grooming a cat can make or break friendships, so start early. Reputable breeders introduce grooming while the kitten is still with its mother. Here is a simple yet effective grooming checklist:

Start with brief grooming sessions.

Increase session times once your cat gets used to short ones.

Learn your cat's limitations. Tail-lashing means your cat has had enough.

Give rewards for good behaviour.

It's a good idea to keep a British Shorthair indoors only to protect him from diseases spread by other cats, attacks by dogs and other dangers that cats face when they go outside, such as being hit by a car. British Shorthairs who go outside are also at risk of being stolen by someone who wants to have such a beautiful cat without paying for it.

Most cats are relatively clean and rarely require bathing, but you should at least brush or comb your cat regularly. Brushing your cat's coat regularly helps to keep it lush, and clean, it also reduces shedding and the likelihood of hairballs.

Diet

There is plenty to choose from since the creation of the first cat food[1] in the 1900s[2]. The British Shorthair, like all cats, benefits from a well-balanced diet high in quality ingredients. Feed your cat in proportion to his age, activity level, and energy level and always use high quality cat food based on the advice you initially receive from your breeder, buy the best food you can afford. With time you will be able to gauge how much food your cat needs. A good guide is, quality dry food throughout the day for your cat to snack on, plenty of fresh water and quality wet food for breakfast and dinner to keep them hydrated. I also usually add a little bit of water with their wet food for extra hydration. Stick with high quality food, these are not usually found in your usual grocery store, and avoid foods that contain high amounts of grains and other fillers in favour of foods that list high quality meat and protein as their main ingredient. Avoid making any sudden changes to your cat's diet in order to prevent a visit to the vet as this can cause diarrhea. Allow your cat access to plenty of fresh, clean water, preferably in a stainless steel or crockery bowl as plastic can cause acne and greasy chins. Finally, do not give your cat milk - it will give them the runs. Cats do not have enough bacteria in their stomach to break down the lactose it contains.

While British Shorthairs aren't typically vocal beggars and don't have the energy to jump onto counters or tables, it's best to avoid teaching them bad habits by feeding them food from your plate at mealtimes. Also, avoid adding pieces of human food or treats to your cat's food as this could encourage your cat to become a picky eater. Once again I'd advise you to always buy high quality, brand-name kitten or cat food. Your breeder or vet will be able to evaluate your new cat or kitten and recommend the best diet for them. What and how much a cat should eat depends on factors such as age, activity level, and health. If in doubt, stick with the guidelines set out by the breeder.

Taurine, an essential amino acid, is required by cats for heart and eye health. The food you choose should be appropriate for your cat's or kitten's life stage. Taurine can be found in well-balanced foods.

You must always provide fresh, clean water and wash and refill your cat's water bowls daily. Treats should account for no more than 5-10% of the diet. Do not feed baby food to a cat or kitten who is refusing to eat or is sick. Please read the labels carefully: Your pet could be poisoned if the baby food contains onion or garlic powder for example.

If your pet's symptoms of anorexia, diarrhea, vomiting, or lethargy persist for more than two days, consult your vet.

Litter Tray

British Shorthairs do well with both open top and closed top cat litter trays. Litter will need to be cleaned often as cats do not like dirty litter. All indoor cats require a litter box, which should be kept quiet and easily accessible. One box per floor is recommended in a multi-level home. Avoid moving the box unless absolutely necessary, and if necessary, show your cat its new location. Remember that cats will not use a dirty, stinky litter box, so scoop the solid waste out of the box at least once a day. Safely dispose of everything dirty and please note that although poop can be flushed never dump dirty litter down the toilet as that will block your pipes. The litter tray can be washed with a mild detergent, and refilled at least once a week. Clumping litter requires less frequent cleaning. When cleaning the litter box, avoid using ammonia, deodorants, or scents, particularly lemon. Please consult your vet if your cat refuses to use a litterbox. When a cat refuses to use a litter box, it may be due to a medical condition that needs treatment.

Use the same kind of litter that your kitten has become accustomed to at the breeder's as changing this too soon can cause unwanted accidents around the house. If you want to change the litter do so slowly by either mixing them slowly or leaving both out. Below is a summary of what you can expect from the many choices of litters available.

Clay Gravel. The cheapest approach. The major issue with clay gravel is that it produces dust and has low moisture and odour absorption.

Green litters. Environmentally friendly and cost effective. The major drawback is that cats might not like the shavings under their feet and refuse to use them.

Absorbing crystals. The silica gel crystals trap urine, allowing for a dry box and easier clean up. This is an expensive option and again, this will depend on how the 'texture' feels for your cat's paws.

Clumping sand. Very popular choice and offers very good moisture and odour control. This expensive option can generate a little bit of dust and has the potential to fly all over the place. Do not flush it down the toilet as accumulation can damage your pipes.

Cats are very clean by nature, so, simply place your kitten in a clean litter box and he will get the idea. Litter visits will vary from kitten to kitten, but on average most cats will need to empty their bladder every 8 -12 hours. Young kittens will be able to hold their bladder and bowels for shorter periods of time and generally will need to use the litter within 10 minutes after eating or drinking. You will notice that you kitten might display some of these signs when in need of the toilet.

- ☐ Sniffing around
- ☐ Meowing
- ☐ Looking for the litter box
- ☐ Looking agitated or crying by the door to get out
- ☐ Squatting

If unable to find the litter, your kitten will most likely choose a soft towel, carpet, bed or sofa for relieving themselves. To prevent further behavior, clean the affected area with bicarb or any specialised cat cleaning products. You might want to reward your kitten with verbal praise and treats every time they get it righ and even give him food in the previously affected area as cats do not use eating areas to relieve themselves. If you catch a kitten making a mistake, say in a calm but fim "No" and take them to their litter or bathroom area.

Litter Training

Toilet training. There are several schools of thought on how to train a cat to use a human toilet. Litter Kwitter and CitiKitty are two training devices that can help you train your adult cat to use the toilet instead of a litter box. However, you must determine whether you want to pursue this road with your cat. It's also a good idea to set up a separate bathroom exclusively for your companion.

Bell Training. You can train your British Shorthair to let you know when they want to go outside to use the litter or your enclosed garden. Hang the bell from the door handle with a piece of string or ribbon. Show them how to ring the bell with their paw. When they ring the doorbell, praise your cat and promptly open the door. The disadvantage of employing this technique is that your cat may begin to use it whenever they are bored and want to go outside.

Bedtding

We've observed that our kittens love sheep skin or doughnut beds as a close alternative. Sheepskin looks and smells great and can be placed anywhere in the house as long it's a place your cat enjoys. Top favourite sleeping places include owner's bed, armchairs, outside in the warm sun, near the radiator, cat bed/basket and owner's lap[3].

Scratching Post

Please ensure your kitten has a scratching post or even a scratching lounge if you would rather have something fancier.

Toys

Concentrate on items that do not pose a choking hazard nor present a possibility of being lethal if swallowed. Many kitten toys will always require supervision. Anything with strings, feathers, bells, or other attached decorations falls into this category. Kittens love anything from paper balls, to activity centres to elaborate scratching posts. Baby play mats or soft baby gyms are also great ways to keep your kitten busy. They go absolutely bonkers playing with these things.

Should I Adopt Two Kittens?

Twice the fun, twice the work. Saying that, if you have the room in your home and can afford the purchase and care I would say yes, go for it. British Shorthair do well in pairs. This will naturally mean double-trouble for the first year or so as kittens go crazy with their play around the house. Litter mates are usually the best option but even kittens from different litter can form a fantastic bond and remain friends for life. Before adopting more than one kitten please consider the following:

- ☐ Do I have the patience to look after two rascals instead of one?
- ☐ Do I have the time and energy to give them constant attention and care?
- ☐ Do I have the finances to provide for more than one kitten?

Bear in mind that this applies to inactive kittens (kittens sold as pets) only as they must be neutered or spayed. I've observed over the years that unneutered or unspayed cats are more territorial and can fight, especially the girls.

Should I Choose A Male Or Female?

In my years of experience this is only a matter of preference as both male and female cats each equally possess the same characteristics. Males tend to be slightly bigger and chubbier perhaps and neutering for male cats is cheaper and less invasive than the spaying procedure required for females. Therefore, the best way to choose a kitten will be to observe them when you visit the breeder.

Cat Language

Meowing

All cats meow for various reasons. Scientists have identified more than a dozen different cat meows, each with their own meaning. Purring, for instance, shows how friendly and content your cat is. As you learn your cat's language you will become more attuned to their different meows and their meanings.

Communication - Meowing upon greeting or anticipation of their favourite food, frustration or purring to show contentment and happiness.

Danger - Meowing upon eminent danger, this can also include growing or howling and agitation.

Attention or Boredom - Your British Shorthair will get up to all sorts of antics to get your attention, from running around the house at the speed of light as they meow to unrolling the entire toilet paper onto the floor. It's important to be patient and stay calm as even negative attention can be rewarding.

Fear or pain - Cats are not very good at showing pain, unless it's severe, at which they may hiss or growl. You may find that they display the same sort of meow when frightened. Fear is also accompanied by spitting, folded ears and crouching.

Tail Twitching

Your British Shorthair will also convey emotions through their tail.

Straight up tail means that your cat is displaying friendship and contentment. Kittens do this with their mother and siblings.

Straight up tail with a hook at the end means that the cat is friendly but not totally sure.

Straight up quivering tail means happiness or, in the case of unneutered males, that he is about to spray.

Straight tail and in the down position means that your cat is in a potentially aggressive mood and as they become more agitated, the tail position may switch to one side or the other.

Dramatic swishing tail usually means that your cat wants to be left alone. The speed of the wag usually indicates how annoyed a cat may be.

Twitching the tail in a seated position means the cat is alert and interested in something that has caught their attention, such as a bird or fish.

Tail carried down and between the legs means that your cat is feeling nervous and submissive.

Fully bristled, straight up tail means that your cat is very angry or has received a fright.

Tail entwining. Sometimes a cat will do this to another cat friend or around your legs to mark their territory, show friendship or get your attention.

Ears Communication

Slightly forward: "I'm very relaxed".
Straight up: "I better stay alert and pay attention!"
Slightly back: " Not sure about that, I am getting slightly annoyed."
Turned right back: "I'm scared!"
Back and flattened against head: "I am really frightened. Better fold my ears back really tight against my head to protect them from claws and teeth. I might need to get ready to fight!"

Eyes Communication

"Please don't stare. It makes me feel uncomfortable and intimidated. Soft, half-closed eyes or slow blinks would make this feeling go away. It shows that you are still my friend and poses no threat to me!"

PART 2: PREPARING YOUR HOME FOR YOUR BRITISH SHORTHAIR

CHAPTER 4

THE SHOPPING LIST

Before you even decide to take your new British Shorthair home, there are certain steps you should take to make your home a more welcoming place for the new family member. Before you bring your new cat or kitten home, there are several things to collect or buy, so your cat will feel like a family member rather than a visitor. Do this a few days in advance to save stress on the big day. in the excitement of bringing your cat home, you don't want to suddenly discover at 11 p.m. that you forgot to buy cat food. Here are the minimum essentials your cat will need:

Food

Assume you can communicate with the cat's previous caregivers. In that case, you should probably feed your new pet whatever they are used to. If you purchase a cat from a breeder, their contract will almost always strongly advise or require you to feed a certain type of food. Here are some pointers to consider when deciding what to feed your cat or kitten if his or her background is unknown:

Kittens. Kittens require more fats and proteins than adult cats, so look for foods that say Complete and Balanced Nutrition on the label, as well as the AAFCO animal feeding, tested statement for all life stages. There are also kitten specific foods on the market. The words highly digestible, nutrient-dense, and uniquely designed to meet the nutritional needs of kittens distinguish these.

Adult cats. Cats generally prefer wet foods, but your cat may be accustomed to only dry food. Dry food is ideal for grown cats, and any premium brand will suffice. You should also supplement your cat's diet with wet food to health them stay hydrated.

Bowls For Food And Water

Although your new cat can be fed in any ceramic (non-lead-glazed) or stainless steel bowls in your kitchen, you may feel more comfortable giving them their own dishes. Plastic dishes are not recommended for cats because they can cause chin rashes in some cats; additionally, softer plastic scratches, providing a breeding ground for bacteria (possibly a case of cause-and-effect here.) There are several non-tip stainless steel bowls for pets available. If you prefer decorated ceramic dishes, make certain that the glaze is free of lead. Automatic food and water servers are especially useful if you will be gone for extended periods during the day, such as to work or school. The pure, fresh taste of running water is preferred by most cats, and automatic water dispensers ensure a constant supply of clean water.

Toys

All cats enjoy playing, and your bonding time will begin with Kitty and her toys. The fishing pole, dangling lure type of toy is a big hit for interactive play. Just make sure it's strong enough that small kittens don't tear off feathers or other decorations from the dangling part. Catnip mice are an all-time favorite. Kitty houses and climbing posts can range from simple cardboard creations to expensive custom-built cat furniture combinations.

Grooming Tools

Grooming time is an excellent opportunity to bond with your cat or new kitten. Look for a fine-toothed comb and a pin brush with a rubber backing. A cat-specific nail clipper is a plus. If you begin clipping your kitten's nails at a young age, it will make the task much easier when she is older. Please refer to www.muffinandpoppy.co.uk for suitable tools.

Pet Carrier

This is an absolute must. Never attempt to transport a cat without one. You'll need a solid-bottomed fiberglass or tough plastic carrier with a secure latch and a screened opening through which the cat can look. If you plan to travel, a heavy-duty cloth airline-approved carrier is a good option.

The Scratching Post

Whether you like it or not, your cat will scratch. Begin your relationship on the right foot by purchasing a scratching post. It can be as simple or as elaborate as you want; if you're handy with tools, you can even assemble one yourself. To attract your cat, some commercially made scratching posts are scented with catnip. If you're on a tight budget, start with a cardboard scratcher.

Litter And Litter Boxes

Selecting the best litter box for your pet is critical for both indoor and indoor-outdoor cats. For grown cats, look for a large box with high sides, as they tend to throw the litter around a lot. These can also be as simple or as elaborate as your budget allows but start with a simple plastic litterbox. Young kittens will need a box that is low enough for them to enter. Consider putting a mat under the box to catch the stray litter. Mats for this purpose can be purchased at a pet store, or you can purchase a few inexpensive carpet or linoleum samples that can simply be tossed and replaced when they become too dirty. Some hooded litter boxes come with something that looks like a black sponge, that's a charcoal filter to go on top of the litter box to filter the air not a cleaning device. It took me years to realise that, after countless occasions where I rinsed out the black diluted remains from the litter boxes after washing it with soap and water. For years I thought they were just bad sponges until my wife pointed out that they were charcoal filters. You live and learn.

A Bed (Optional, But Recommended)

If this is your first cat, they will most likely sleep in your bed. However, it's still a good idea to give your cat their own special, cozy napping spot. The bed should be comfortable, easy to clean, and large enough for an adult cat to curl up comfortably, but not so large that she feels exposed and vulnerable.

Make A Vet Appointment

This isn't exactly a shopping list item. Still, unless your cat comes with papers proving a recent veterinary visit and proof of vaccinations, your first stop should be at your local veterinary clinic before even bringing them home.

CHAPTER 5

KITTEN PROOFING YOUR HOME

One of the most important things to do before bringing a new kitten home is to set up a safe room for your new bundle of energy to spend the first few days in. It should include everything a kitten requires for comfort and security. Although a separate room is required if there are other cats in the house, a safe room does not always need to be separate. If this is the only pet in the house, the safe room could even be a section of a larger room. This will make your kitten feel at ease. It's important to make sure that power cords are tucked away securely out of your kitten's reach or inside a chew-proof PVC tube as they look like irresistible, fun toys to hyper-and-eager-to-explore teething kittens.

Kitten Proofing Checklist

Living Room. Check for tempting electrical wires, chewable items, precious (climbable) curtains, silk throws or anything that can be easily knocked down during a playing frenzy such as your latest model flat screen TV. Your lovable furball of energy will calm down as he gets older but for now it's better to be safe than sorry.

Office. Watch out for unattended open windows, electrical cords, choking hazards such as paper clips, elastic bands. British Shorthairs tend to try and copy us so if they see you typing on your laptop keyboard they will try to copy you and remove some keys by accident while they type, encouraging you to get the old one replaced. Believe me, when I say this.

Bathroom. Equally if you are really close to your cats and decide that you don't mind if they are around when you pay a visit to the outhouse don't be surprised if they also decide to go for the toilet paper after using their litter even if it's just to roll the whole thing out of its frame.

Believe me. Don't be surprised.

On a more serious note, be vigilant to keep everything in its safe place, watch out for razors and shaving devices, wires, cotton swabs, jewellery, medicine and open bins. Anything toxic or that could cause a choking problem should be put away safely.

Bedroom. Keep items such as shoe strings, slippers and clothing in its appropriate place or you may find that your ever-playful friend has claimed your new Louis Vuitton sunglasses for their new playing spot. Wherever that may be.

Kitchen. Food glorious food! I am sure I can almost hear them singing the tune everytime we find ourselves in the kitchen. You can see it in their eyes. The excitement. The gusto. Not because they are hungry. No, because this is that magical place where amazing nibbles are made. Open the fridge and here comes a slice of salmon. Yummy! Although your British Shorthair is very smart it's always better to be safe than sorry. Make sure that empty dishes have been safely placed on the counter and check the kitchen for leftovers or anything that could represent danger such as extremely sharp knives and hot stoves. The kitchen disposable bin must also be securely shut and never feed your cat random food as you might be poisoning him instead of nourishing. See Appendix B for a list of foods that can seriously harm or kill your cats.

Garage. Dangers include antifreeze, petrol (gasoline), fertilizers, any form of poison, cleaners. If your cat has access to this area, keep everything stored inside a locked cabinet.

Garden. Do not allow your cat access to the outside area if you use toxic chemicals or poison anywhere is your garden.

Plants. Do you have plants in your house? If so, please check Appendix A for a list of poisonous plants. Lilies make the top of the list. If you have them in your house, dispose of them as soon as possible as they are highly poisonous to your British Shorthair.

Before you begin think about the best room (or area) in your home that can work for a safe room. You want it to be closed off from the rest of the house. Most kittens will be curious and eager to explore their new home to its full extent, which means that they will get into everything within reach and magically disappear from sight. Little objects will all of a sudden create (fluffy) little legs and mysteriously disappear too. This includes jaw guards, reading glasses, cash - you've been warned.

Suppose the kitten's perfect room has two tall screens to create a private section in an unused corner of long blinds. In that case, you may want to remove them or tie them up while the room is being used by the new high-octane tiny bundle of joy. Be sure that everyone in your house knows that this area or room is temporarily being used by the new house owner, which means eliminating all sources of danger, as you would do for a curious toddler. Be mindful that your kitten will want to touch, sniff, taste and chew every electrical cord, closet, open pipes, fireplace and anything you may have left lying on the floor.

For your kittens comfort spend some time gathering these supplies for your safe room,

- ☐ Litter box and scoop.
- ☐ Scratching post.
- ☐ Cat bed or tower.
- ☐ Stainless steel or ceramic food and water bowls
- ☐ Plenty of toys
- ☐ A dividing screen or two if you have to use the corner of a room

Litter Box Placement

Place the litter box in a room corner, away from the food and water bowls. It doesn't have to be anything fancy. The most important thing is that it is the correct size for your cat. If you want to hide it, many nice litter box covers look like furniture. Some cats, however, may refuse to use a covered litter box, so if your new cat goes to the bathroom in the middle of the room, you may need to remove it. You'll also need a scoop and a container for the scoopings.

Scratching Post Placement

Place the scratching post relatively close to your cat's bed as they normally like to scratch and stretch the moment they wake up. Make sure it's a good sturdy one. Most cats prefer sisal covering over carpet. This will help to reduce the chances of your cat scratching your furniture. You could consider a cat tower as an alternative if you have enough space and the budget to do so as most of these have sisal around their columns. Furthermore, because of their innate attraction to high places, many cats prefer a tower to a bed with a nice platform at the top.

Sleeping Place

Cats require a comfortable, private place to sleep because they sleep for most of the day. They frequently prefer to sleep on high perches such as windowsills, shelves, and furniture tops but in the absence of a tower a donut bed or sheep skin will also do. Of course, if the safe room is in a bedroom, your new cat may quickly disregard the nice little bed you purchased in favor of the human bed.

Water and Food

Food and water bowls should be kept at a safe distance from the litter box. They are typically made of glass, stainless steel, or ceramic.

Toys

It's a good idea to have a few toys around your new British Shorthair safe haven. You'll need at least one interactive cat toy for bonding purposes, as well as one or two play-alone toys for when you're not around. Treat-dispensing toys are a great way to keep your cat physically and mentally stimulated. It's a good idea to stock up on extra toys and rotate them out regularly.

Preventing Issues

The safe room's purpose is to keep your new cat contained in a secure environment. It's not terrible, but it's not ideal if your new cat escapes and roams around your house. Houses are full of dangers, so as soon as you realize the cat has escaped, try to return it to the safe room. All play should begin in the safe room and gradually progress to the rest of the house in timed increments. If you introduce your kitten to an older cat in your home, a bigger problem may arise. Prevent the older cat from visiting the safe room and slowly and positively establish a friendship by allowing them to eat together, perhaps each on a different side of the door to begin with and then under supervision when the appropriate time arrives.

Last Minute Tips

Before bringing your cat home, make sure to cat-proof the entire area. To keep stray litter from landing on the carpet or floor, you'll need something under the litter box. Litter mats are designed for this purpose, but a layer of newspaper will do in a pinch. Toys made from rolled-up newspaper wads are also suitable for interactive fetch games. Also, a soft pillow that has seen better days can serve as a suitable substitute for a cat bed.

Why Kitten Proof Your Home

Kittens are small animals with a keen sense of curiosity, a keen sense of smell, and an unexpected ability to leap, crawl, and use their claws. As a result, kittens are more likely to get themselves into dangerous situations—or to damage your delicate decorations or fancy dinner. Kittens are fascinated by anything that moves and by almost anything that they can move with their paws. This includes wires, trinkets, bathroom accessories, and tablecloths. Some of these items can be hazardous to kittens, while others are easily broken. Kittens adore climbing and will scale almost any structure. If they can, they'll also sneak through open doors and windows. Kittens require sharpening of their claws and enjoy stretching their claws. This is fine as long as they aren't ripping your favorite clothes or expensive carpet. Kittens have noses close to the ground and, like human babies, enjoy putting things in their mouths. Rubbish is not an exception. Kittens can't tell human food from cat food or safe treats from potentially harmful foods, so they can leap, climb, and zip past you without making a sound—and you've got a good idea of the task ahead of you.

Look around your house first, at high shelves and low cupboards and hidden nooks. Could the kitten get onto a shelf holding valuable or fragile items? Could they become trapped inside a cupboard?

If you're into needlework, keep your supplies in a closed container. Needles and thread might appear to be fine playthings but can be fatal if your kitten swallows them. If you want to use yarn as a kitten toy, carefully put it away after your play session.

Fold and secure your window blinds cord with a rubber band out of the your kittens reach. If she gets tangled up in it, she could strangle.

Kittens will pick up almost anything they can and love knocking over rubbish bins. If you don't want to find your floors littered with waste, invest in covered bin baskets and kitchen disposal containers.

Always keep the door to your washing machine and dryer closed, and double-check inside before using it. Cats like to find dark, warm places to sleep, and the results could be tragic.

Keep the floor clean of stray rubber bands, ribbons, and twine. All are hazardous when ingested by a kitten.

Cover any food you leave out, as kittens have terrific noses and will be attracted to all kinds of treats. Be especially careful with foods that can be harmful to kittens; chocolate, for example, is toxic to cats.

Cloth drapes are better left out of reach of your furry curtain-climber spider-cat. Tie them up securely until your kitten is trained to a scratching post.

Keep your toilet lid down at all times, lest your kitten falls in or drink from it.

Do not keep your kitten in the garage, and always keep the doors closed. Antifreeze is very tasty to animals and is just one of the common poisonous substances found in garages.

Cover electric cords, such as the tangle from your computer, with covers sold for that purpose.

There are several household plants poisonous to cats. Floral arrangements can also be dangerous, so check before putting flowers in locations where cats can reach them.

Use animal-safe insect repellent. Insect poison can harm your cat if ingested.

First Week Checklist

Before Collection

- [ ] Full payment cleared.
- [ ] Signed spaying/neutering agreement.
- [ ] Kitten care guide from breeder.
- [ ] Pen and paper or digital device with extra questions or space for notes.
- [ ] Transfer of keepership form to record the microchipped kitten to your name.
- [ ] Insurance pre-activation documentation and/or terms of service.
- [ ] Kitten safe area clean and ready.
- [ ] Off-limit zones shut.
- [ ] Windows shut.
- [ ] Kitten hazards out of kitten's reach.
- [ ] Pet carrier. It is not advisable to hold your kitten during the journey.
- [ ] Pee pads for long journeys.
- [ ] Pet carrier securely fastened to the seat of the vehicle.

First Night

- [ ] Introduce your kitten to its new home.
- [ ] Show where the litter box is.
- [ ] Show where the food and water bowl is.
- [ ] Show your kitten where its comfy bed is.
- [ ] Have toys and a scratching post available.
- [ ] First Week
- [ ] Have a consistent waking up and feeding routine. Cats thrive on routine.
- [ ] Scheduled consistent play sessions to bond with your kitten.

Mistakes To Avoid

Sleeping in your bed. While this may help to calm and comfort your kitten it will also train your cat to only sleep in your bed. Also little kittens can potentially get hurt by a sleeping human body.

Comforting at the wrong time. Avoid picking your kitten up if it displays nervousness, fear or aggression towards a person, other pets or objects as this will reward them for unbalanced behaviour.

Codependency. Carrying your kitten everywhere instead of using a leash might encourage your cat to become possessive and co-dependant.

Rough play. Kittens don't usually appreciate when humans play too hard or rough with them. Children should be taught to play appropriately with young kittens and they must allow them to rest.

Hand play. Always discourage your kitten from biting your hands or any part of your body. Making a fist removing the enticing human fingers combined with a firm no should discourage such activity as chewing and biting will only get harder as your kitten gets older.

No grooming routine. No regular brushing, claw clipping, teeth brushing and even bathing will only lead to a lifetime of trauma for you and your kitten every time these procedures must be performed.

No feeding routine. Your cat needs a feeding routine as much as we humans do.

No discipline. When your kitten tries something that you disapprove of you must firmly tell them "No", and distract them with an alternative. If biting your hand for example, offer them a toy. Distraction and replacement can be powerful training tools. Don't forget to happily praise your kitten everytime it does something right but if it persists on chewing your hand then walk away or allow your kitten to have some down time inside the pet carrier until it calms down. Always praise your kitten for acceptable behaviour or replace inappropriate behaviour with what is acceptable to you.

Not bonding with your kitten. Bonding starts from the very moment when you put your kitten in your pet carrier. At this point you will have the opportunity to softly calm him down and get them used to your voice. When you arrive home be patient and gentle as they start to adapt to a whole new environment. Reserve daily quality time with your kitten such as grooming, walks (if you choose to leash train them), play sessions and hanging out by sitting on the couch watching TV or reading a book.

CHAPTER 6

HELPING YOUR KITTEN ADJUST TO THE NEW LIFE

The best advice on helping your highly adaptable British Shorthair kitten make a smooth transition to life with you will come directly from the breeder. Your kitten should grow into an easygoing companion with a steady nature. At first, you will want to keep your kitten confined to a more contained area completely separated from other pets. The best initial introduction with other pets are those conducted via sniffing under the door or through the per carrier. Safety is the key here. Face-to-face encounters should be done safely under supervision, perhaps a leach can be used at this stage. Do not be nervous as they will pick up on your emotions. Food can also be safely introduced as you want your pets to associate their encounter to good things. If a rescue is necessary, do so calmly. Most cats will take two to four weeks to get used to their new surroundings and don't be surprised if your little furball quickly shoots up to the pecking order. If your kitten is outside, make sure your enclosed garden is free of snail poison, rodent traps, and other potentially hazardous materials. Better yet, surround him with appealing toys and confine him to your home. It can be a thrilling experience to welcome a new British Shorthair into your family. It can be a stressful time for the cat as well. It may take some time for thcm to adjust to their new surroundings, but there are several things you can do to help reduce stress during this time. If you work, taking some time off during this transition period can make a huge difference in assisting your cat in settling in more smoothly.

What to Expect Throughout The Adoption Process

Adopting a cat can be a very rewarding experience. You are providing a home for a new pet, and it can warm your heart to see them come out of their shell and enjoy life. When you rehome from a reputable rescue organization, you will receive the appropriate level of support before, during, and after adoption. It also implies that your cat received proper health checks, temperament assessments, and support during their stay with them. Don't be offended if the organization wants to come to your house for a home inspection or if they ask you a lot of questions about your living situation and lifestyle. It's great that they want to put their cats in the right kind of home.

Why Taking a Break From Work Can Benefit Your New Cat

While many people understand the value of taking some time off to help a dog adjust to their new home, it is often assumed that cats will do just fine without as much assistance due to their more independent nature. A cat's adjustment to a new home environment can be extremely stressful. Being present to help them settle in can reduce their stress, help them settle in faster, and contribute to developing a strong bond between you and your new housemate. The first 24 to 48 hours can be the most stressful for your cat; make sure you monitor things during this time. Some things you can do to help in the early stages is to *make a safe haven for your cat*. This is extremely important and is frequently overlooked. Allowing your cat unrestricted access to the entire house can be intimidating. It is far preferable to set up a cat-proofed, quiet, and secure room to use as a safe space when they first arrive. This should be their safe haven for at least the first day. Allow no other pets or loud children into the room. *Supervision* during this time is also essential. If you are away from home from the moment your cat arrives, not only will it be more difficult to form a strong bond, but you will also be unable to see if they are distressed, confused, or even mischievous. Perhaps all you need to do is remind them of the litter box or feeding bowls location. Some cats may feel more at ease with your presence in the room. If you have a cat that is quickly settling in but is a bit of a rogue, you may need additional steps to cat-proof the house. Do they need to be directed to a scratch post rather than the sofa corners? When they start exploring the countertops, you may need to relocate some ornaments. Cats can be extremely territorial. Introductions with any other cats in the household must be carefully supervised and done gradually. If you are present during the first days of introductions, you will be able to intervene if things are not going well.

By staying at home and spending time with your cat, you will increase the chances of relaxing and bonding with your kitten from the start.

Building Trust: How To Establish A Good Relationship With Your New Cat

You may find that your new cat immediately seeks out a hiding spot. Don't try to force them out of that space. When you do go into the room, try not to move about or make too much noise. Your time off could be the perfect time to catch up on that book you wanted to read.

If your cat starts to come out of its hiding spot, let them initiate any contact. Have a bag of tasty treats nearby. If they take them, verbally praise them for the interaction.

If they retreat again to their hiding spot, be patient and let them come out again when they are ready. This could be within hours; others may take days before they venture out with confidence. Patience is key here.

Once they are more comfortable in their space and happy with you being around, you can gradually introduce other family members. If you have young children, make sure they know the rules. The cat's room is a quiet space; they should not chase the cat or sit next to their hiding spot. They should only interact if the cat comes to them.

Once your cat is fully relaxed you can gradually introduce them to other areas of the house.

Being around 24/7 for the first few days or weeks of your cat's arrival will help you to supervise, react, interact and build a strong bond for years to come.

Setting Up The Litter Box

Poor litter box hygiene is frequently to blame for a cat's mishaps. Cats despise dirty litter boxes and may be compelled to seek alternatives, such as a corner of the carpet or a basket of clean laundry in the closet. Because your cat's sense of smell is 14 times stronger than yours, a litter box that smells clean to you may stink to your cat. While automated litter boxes are becoming more popular, their costs are prohibitively expensive for many cat owners. Many cats prefer traditional litter boxes. As a general rule, a household should provide one litter box for each cat resident, plus one extra. If you have more than three litter boxes, you'll probably run out of logical places to put them. A litter station with two or three boxes side by side can house more than one cat at once (as long as the cats tolerate it). It will also make scooping and cleaning up a little easier. The choice of the litter box and cleaning products are very personal, and the one size fits all rule rarely applies. The most important thing is to follow the breeder's advice. Also. cats will notify you if they are dissatisfied with your litter boxes and accessory products.

What You'll Need

☐ Wastebasket or disposal bin for dirty litter
☐ Cleaning cloth

☐ Litter box liners (optional)
☐ Litter
☐ Unscented dish soap or pet safe cleaning solution

Unless your cat prefers covered boxes or the box is in an area where you want to keep it hidden, such as the kitchen, a plain rectangular box is the best place to start. Make sure the box is large enough for your cat to move around in and has no overhang. The box should be placed away from noisy appliances for maximum privacy. If you have a cat who likes to bully other cats, it should have an easy escape route. Being trapped in his litter box will undoubtedly frighten the cat and may cause him to avoid using the box in the future.

The use of litter box liners is optional, but they are useful for neatly disposing of the used litter when it is time to empty and wash the box. Liners are a significant benefit when using non-scooping litter because they contain the excess urine that starts to accumulate, which is why most non-scooping litter must be changed regularly.

The majority of cat litter manufacturers recommend two to three inches of litter. If your cats are deep scratchers who will dig to the bottom of the litter box if you use less, you may want to use three to four inches. Begin with two inches and work your way up until you find the perfect depth for your cat. After you've finished filling the litter box, level it off, so the cats have a nice, smooth surface to dig in.

Scooping is simple with clumping litter because urine clumps into fairly solid chunks that can be scooped out while sifting the clean litter back into the box. The litter coats the poop, preventing it from sticking to the scoop. The litter box should be scooped at least twice daily and more frequently if necessary. After scooping, you may need to add new litter to replace the amount that was lost. Using clumping litter, you regularly scoop to keep the litter box smelling fresh and clean. Still, the box will need to be emptied and thoroughly cleaned at some point. Depending on the type of litter you use, this could be every week or every four or five weeks. Non-clumping litter must be emptied and washed much more frequently, owing to urine accumulation at the bottom of the box. The odor quickly becomes overpowering. Empty the used litter into a strong plastic bag and tie it securely before throwing it away. It should be noted that, while some natural litters are flushable, it's not advisable to do so as your drain could eventually get damaged. The litter tray can then be washed with unscented dish soap and hot water. Rinse thoroughly, then pat dry with paper towels or cleaning cloths.

Learning To Play With Your Cat

The majority of people enjoy watching their cats stalk, pounce and play.

Cats are extremely intelligent, naturally curious, and active animals. We must ensure that they receive adequate mental and physical stimulation. Your British Shortahir must be able to hunt, stalk, and engage in natural, instinctive behaviors. Give them appropriate resources to play with, allow them to engage in natural predatory behaviors, and give them control over social interactions. Here are some suggestions for cat-friendly play in your home. Make sure you have various toys and items that simulate or mimic the prey that cats hunt naturally.

Toys that have erratic movements and simulate or mimic the movements of prey are very exciting to cats. Rotate and change your cat's toys on a routine basis to keep them interested. Some cats become bored with a toy after a few days, some a few weeks, and some prefer only one toy. Allow your cat to capture the prey at the end of their play session to satisfy their natural hunting instinct. This also prevents your cat from becoming frustrated. While lasers are very attractive to most cats, they don't allow your cat to feel the sense of accomplishment of capturing the prey.

TIP: Hide a treat or piece of kibble if you use a laser. Finally, allow your cat to capture the laser where the treat is hidden. In this manner, he feels as if he has captured the prey and is rewarded.

When cats are hungry, they tend to play more. So keep an eye on their weight, feed him small, frequent meals, and even hide food around the house to encourage them to play more. To entice your cat, put dry food in food puzzles. This type of feeding simulates hunting and can help overweight cats lose weight. Toys and enrichment items such as cat trees, perches, and windows to watch outdoor activity should be available for your cat to play alone when you are not present. You can also make your own cat toys out of common household items such as, paper towel rolls, boxes, socks, cardboard and crumpled paper. Your cat has finished playing when he walks away from you. Instead of forcing interaction, allow them to initiate, select, and control the type of human contact they desire. Each cat has a different preference for how much human interaction they want.

Use interactive toys that mimic prey, such as a toy mouse, to encourage your cat to play. You can move the toy around by pulling it across the floor or waving a feather wand through the air.

When playing with your cat, avoid using string-type products. String, yarn, and similar products such as rubber bands, tinsel, ribbon, streamers, and so on are easily swallowed and can cause severe intestinal problems that necessitate surgery.

If the toys or products contain loose parts (bells, googly eyes, small pieces) or string-type materials that your cat can swallow, store them safely after playtime. These materials can be found in a variety of household items and children's toys. It is critical to keep an eye on all items brought into your home and store anything hazardous to your cat.

Introduce interactive play early in your cat's life so he can learn how to play with you and never use your hands or feet as toys during play. Although it may seem cute with kittens, as your kitten grows into a cat, he will believe this is an appropriate form of play. Believe me you don't want those *wolverine* claws piercing your skin.

Use food puzzles or food balls to mimic hunting for prey and provide a more natural eating behavior. It can also help your cat eat more slowly as he needs to work for their food.

Reward your cat with treats to provide positive reinforcement. If you have more than one cat, remember to play with them individually.

Teach children and those unfamiliar with cats how to play appropriately with your cats. This will help prevent your cats from becoming frustrated or scared.

Play also provides your cat with much-needed exercise. Exercise is critical in maintaining a healthy body weight and preventing your cat from becoming overweight or obese. When it comes to playtime any type of wand toy with dangling attachments or even paper balls will do as they would rather play with you than wait for an expensive item from the pet store. My eldest cat loves playing fetch with a paper ball. He will actually chase the ball and bring it to me for another round. It's his favourite game to play apart from chasing little things. If your cat ever develops an unhealthy interest in your furniture, you can discourage their behaviour by using pennyroyal or orange essence sprays and even double-sided adhesive strips.

Make sure your cat has plenty of safe places to hide. This gives him a place to go when he needs to be alone. Tall-sided or igloo cat beds, as well as cardboard boxes, are excellent choices. Cats enjoy elevated perches or cat trees because they allow them to observe, feel safe, and, well, feel superior. Your cat requires scratching posts to express their natural scratching behavior. Include scratching areas in your home for them to sharpen their claws and stretch their muscles. Be sure you place your cat's litter boxes where they can easily access them without any challenges or potential threats. Place his food and water in a separate area where they can eat and drink without stress. In general, the more cats you have in a household, the more perches, hiding areas, and feeding and drinking areas you'll need so each cat can feel independent and comfortable in their home domain.

How To Play With Kittens

Kittens will play with whatever they can get their paws on. Remember that your kitten is a baby, and you must keep it away from sharp or small objects that it could choke on. Soft objects that kittens can sink their teeth into without hurting themselves, such as cotton chew toys, are the best toys for them. Ideally, a kitten will have other kittens to play with, but if you live in a single-cat household, make sure your kitten isn't being trained to play with your hands or feet. When your kitten grows up and develops full-sized teeth and claws, you'll be glad you've set limits.

How To Play With Adult Cats

Keep a rotating array of toys on hand. Some good cat toys you can buy are wand toys, catnip mice, and crinkly catnip things. Some great toys you already have at home: wads of paper, straws, and plastic rings from milk or juice containers. Put the toys away after playtime. If a toy is always out, it can become boring and unrealistic, like a mouse that never goes away. Make the toy act like a mouse or a bird to pique your cat's curiosity. But let your cat set the pace. You can't force a cat into playing, but you can try different approaches to see what generates interest. You might try dimming the lights since cats like to hunt when it's darker. Match the action intensity to your cat's interest. After a while, you'll get to know your cat's playing style and the look that says, "I'm ready to play!"

PART 3: CARING FOR YOUR BRITISH SHORTHAIR

CHAPTER 7

DAILY DIET

I've observed that the British Shorthair is not a fussy eater. Follow the breeder's advice and you should be just fine. However, some might have strong preferences for menu items such as salmon and tuna for example (which is great for training purposes), while others will abhor the whole idea and stick to their usual diet.

Wet And Dry Food

The best choice for your British Shorthair is to feed a healthy mixture of wet and dry food that provides not only the correct mixture of nutrients but also the tastes and textures your pet will enjoy.

Dry Food
- Must be available throughout the day for your kitten to snack on.
- Easy to serve.
- Easier litter box maintenance.

Wet Food
- Provides a vital source of hydration.
- Cats fed wet food are less prone to gain weight than those who only receive dry food.
- Feed in the morning and before you go to bed to help your cat sleep with a nice full tummy preventing unnecessary sleep deprivation.

Select Balanced Foods

Chances are your breeder has already recommended a top brand of cat food for your new friend. But what if your cat does not come from a reputable breeder? It is helpful for cat owners to know how to read a cat food label. People tend to focus on ingredients but nutrients, particularly protein and fat, are more important. According to Julie A. Churchill, DVM, PhD, associate professor of nutrition at the University of Minnesota College of Veterinary Medicine, it's fashionable to criticize grains and carbohydrates in pet food, but these aren't always bad. Furthermore, food consisting solely of protein and fat becomes very expensive. Carbohydrates can be useful for holding dry food together and making food more affordable, and many cats enjoy the crunch. It's fine as long as the carbs are in a quantity that cats can handle. You will also find that if you invest in quality food there will be no need to give your cat additional vitamins or supplements; the food contains everything they require. What is the best way to tell if your cat's food is balanced? Look for a statement from the Association of American Feed Control Officials (AAFCO) or the Food Standards Agency (FSA) and Defra on the package if you are in the UK[1].

Quantity And Frequency

Most cats will eat their main meals at dawn and dusk when they would normally be hunting and catching prey in the wild, so feeding them at these times is often the best option. The amount of food your cat should have in their bowl depends on their age, size, and activity level, but the average is about 200 calories per day. It's a good idea to check with your breeder or enlist the assistance of your vet in calculating your cat's nutritional requirements. What about treats? treats are fine but should be no more than 5% to 10% of your cat's daily calories.

Vegetables And Food Made From Scratch

Vegetarian or vegan diets may be good for you, but they are not good for your cat. Unlike dogs and humans, cats require specific vitamins, minerals, and proteins that can only be obtained from meat. Raw meat, however, is not ideal. That may be a natural part of life for big cats in the wild, but it is unnatural for house cats. They eat the complete animal or bird, not just the meat, that they catch in the wild. If ingested alone, the meat will be insufficient in vitamins, minerals, and amino acids. Furthermore, bacteria found on raw meat, such as Toxoplasma Gondii, salmonella and E. coli, can make your cat very sick. Avoid single-protein diet such as tuna which may cause severe liver problems. A muscle meat-only-diet will lead to decalcification of the bones. When choosing food ingredients for your cat, always choose products fit for human consumption[2]. If you are considering making your own cat food at home my best advice is for you to refer to Appendix C for a homemade recipe or seek the assistance of a veterinary nutritionist. Cats weigh only 8 to 10 pounds, and changing just one ingredient can drastically alter the nutritional value of the diet. The beauty of commercial food is that it is specifically formulated for cats, so it is complete and balanced and meets their needs, and you don't have to worry about it.

Feeding Mistake To Avoid

Humans are not great at sticking to a healthy balanced diet so it's no surprise that we can also make mistakes when feeding our pets. Our cats are unable to communicate with us through words. Until our cat becomes unwell, we don't usually know where we've gone wrong. Below are some mistakes we commonly make when feeding our beloved companions.

Too Much Food

Overfeeding is probably the most common mistake individuals make while feeding cats, according to professor of medicine and nutrition Joe Bartges. The most frequent nutritional disease in cats is obesity. Obesity is associated with cat health issues such as diabetes, arthritis, and urinary tract disease, even though a fat kitten may appear cuddly and cute. So, how much food should your cat eat? A professional can best answer this question, but recommendations range from 24 to 35 calories per day per pound to keep cats at a normal, healthy weight. However, many of us have no idea what normal looks like. Ask your vet to help you determine your cat's body condition score as they will be able to recognize any weight problems.

Feeding Only Dry Food

A cat's thirst sensitivity is reduced when compared to a dog. They don't drink water voluntarily like dogs do. And because cats naturally produce highly concentrated urine, when their diet is low in liquids, we're setting them up for urinary tract problems. To prevent this I would recommend you feed your British Shorthair wet food (about 78% water while dry food is between 5% and 10%) at least twice a day depending on their age. I also tend to add water to the wet food pouch and pour it back into their bowl for extra hydration.

Providing Insufficient Water

Water is essential for your British Shorthair. According to ASPCA experts, water accounts for 60 to 70% of an adult cat's body weight. A severe water shortage can have serious consequences, resulting in serious illness or death.

Your cat will always require plenty of fresh, clean water. Water benefits your cat, according to the Cornell University College of Veterinary Medicine's website[3]:

Control your body temperature.

Food digestion

Get rid of waste.

Allows salt and other electrolytes to pass through the body while lubricating tissue.

Place several bowls of varying depths around the house to encourage your cat to drink water. Many cats enjoy the sound of running water and fountains are available at most pet stores.

Going Vegetarian or Vegan

Never attempt to convert your cat to a vegetarian or vegan diet. Cats are carnivores, which means they must eat mostly meat and animal organs to survive. Taurine, for example, can only be found in animal tissue. A taurine deficiency can cause heart problems, blindness, and even death in cats. Another advice is to never add garlic to your cat's diet to prevent or combat worms or parasites. It does not work and, if given in excess, garlic can destroy a cat's red blood cells. Do not treat your cat's worms yourself, you may end up doing more harm than good if you use the wrong medication.

Feeding Unbalanced Homemade Diet

There is a growing interest in homemade food for cats. However, it is important to remember that homemade does not always imply health. That's because some people fail to balance the meat with the proper amount of calcium when making cat food from scratch, forgetting that a cat would be eating both the meat and bones of their prey, which provides a proper calcium-to-phosphorus ratio. Too much tuna, liver, or liver oil (such as cod liver oil) in a cat's diet can cause vitamin A toxicosis, which causes bone and joint pain, brittle bones, and dry skin. A diet high in raw fish can deplete vitamin B1, resulting in muscle weakness, seizures, and brain damage[4].

Feeding Dangerous Human Foods

We eat many things that a cat should not eat due to their toxicity in the feline system. These items include, but are not limited to:

alcoholic beverages

avocados

grapes / raisins

eggs

garlic
onions
chives
yeast dough
caffeine in any form
raisins
chocolate

The toxic elements present in chocolate are substances called methylxanthines, which are found in cacao seeds. A similar extract is used in soft beverages, which a cat should never be allowed to consume as they also contain sweeteners that include xylitol, which can cause liver failure. Cats that have been exposed to chocolate or to soft beverages can exhibit symptoms that are severe to the point of being life-threatening. These may include excessive thirst, panting, vomiting, diarrhea, irregular heartbeat, seizures and tremors.

Salty foods are equally dangerous as they can cause rapid dehydration, creating a serious health risk.

Avoid milk. It will give your cat diarrhea as they are lactose intolerant. Felines do not produce sufficient amounts of the enzyme lactase. This means they do not efficiently digest cow's milk and are subject to gastrointestinal upset and diarrhea if they are given too much dairy content in their diets. Adult cats do not require milk, and won't get a lot of nutritional value from consuming it. As a rule of thumb never give your cat milk, believe me, a cat with diarrhoea is not a fun sight, remember they have access to most places in the house.

The best thing to do is to stick with high quality cat food. When you read the label of the food you are considering for your British Shorthair, never lose sight of the fact that cats are meat-eaters. If the first item on the label is not meat, look at another food. Cheaper foods tend to contain much more plant material as filler, while the more expensive or premium foods have a greater amount of meat. With so many kinds of cat food on the market it's always best to go with what the breeder recommends.

Feeding Dairy Food

We have all seen cute drawings of kittens licking a saucer full of milk. What the images never show is the subsequent mess that follows when a cat gets diarrhea the most common symptom of lactose intolerance in cats most likely to occur within 8 to 12 hours after consumption. It's important to understand that while most cats enjoy a little milk, milk does not always reciprocate the affection. The main culprit is lactose, which many cats have difficulty digesting. Cats, like humans, can be lactose intolerant. This is completely normal. Lactase, a milk sugar, must be digested by the enzyme lactase in the digestive systems of humans and cats. This enzyme is abundant in our bodies at birth, and it aids our survival on our mother's milk. However, it is normal for humans and cats to produce less lactase as they age. Lactase deficiency means less ability to digest lactose and lactose intolerance may develop as a result. When a lactose-intolerant cat drinks milk, the undigested lactose passes through the intestinal tract, drawing water with it. Undigested sugars are also fermented by bacteria in the colon, resulting in volatile fatty acids. Saying that, most people have probably given their cats a small amount of milk and never noticed anything wrong. This is because some cats tolerate milk quite well. How do you know? Give your cat a tablespoon or two of milk. If you don't notice any symptoms within a day, chances are your cat will be fine with milk as a treat. A cat who cannot tolerate milk may tolerate other forms of dairy, such as yogurt or cheese. This is because different forms of dairy food contain varying amounts of lactose or they may also be cultured, which means that microorganisms digested some of the lactose. Remember that treats of any kind, such as tuna, meat, cheese, or other human food, should make up no more than 5% to 10% of your cat's diet. The remaining calories in your cat's diet should come from high-quality, nutritionally complete cat food. Personally I would not recommend you give your adult cat any form of milk. Cats do not require milk, and the risks far outweigh the benefits. Furthermore, cow's milk is completely inadequate for kittens. Though kittens have lactase in their systems, it is insufficient to combat the lactose overload found in cow's milk. You can use a kitten-specific milk replacer if your kitten is still young and needs mother's milk. Veterinarians and pet retailers frequently sell cat milk replacers that contain cow's milk that has been processed to mimic the nutrient makeup of cat's milk as precisely as possible. If you're fostering or raising an orphaned kitten, milk replacers developed specifically for kittens are a great option.

Diet For A Healthy Coat

The shiny coat of a British Shorthair is beautiful, a pleasure to touch, and extremely beautiful. A cat's coat can have up to 130,000 hairs per square inch. British Shorthairs are reported to have more fur per square inch than any other cat breed. Surprisingly, other than brushing or combing with a wire toothed comb to remove dead and loose hairs, this luxuriant coat takes relatively little maintenance. To reduce shedding, this should be done once a week. And these hairs can do a variety of things:

- They provide sensory information to cats.
- They shield it from extreme heat and cold, as well as wind and rain.
- They even assist a cat in the production of essential nutrients such as vitamin D.

As previously mentioned, British Shorthair cats are low maintenance when comes to their fur as they always seem to look posh and lush without much attention. Saying that, various factors can cause your cat's coat to become dull or its skin to become dry and flaky. Among the most common causes are:

Inadequate Nutrition

Your British Shorthair, requires a diet rich in carbohydrates, proteins, and fats for healthy hair, skin, and body. If your cat only consumes low-quality, difficult-to-digest food, he or she may become deficient in essential minerals and vitamins. Your cat's skin and coat reflect what's going on inside its body. When the fur becomes dull, or the skin becomes dry one of the first thing we may need to look at is the diet. To maintain a healthy physique and lustrous hair, cats require substantially more protein, complex carbs, and good fats than dogs. A low-fat diet or one that consists mostly of low-quality, generic foods will almost certainly result in a poor-quality coat. The most reasonable remedy, is to switch to a premium brand of cat food. You can also try adding fatty acids like those found in salmon or other fish oils to your cat's food. The results are expected to take about four to six weeks. I would usually stick with the food the breeder recommends and would advise you to consult your veterinarian before changing your cat's food or commencing any supplement regimen.

Weight Problems

When cats gain weight, they lose the ability to clean their entire body. This can result in a lifeless, unkempt coat. Is your cat suffering from dandruff on its back or around the base of its tail? That could indicate that they're unable to reach these areas because they are overweight or obese. Being overweight doesn't just make your cat less flexible. Excess weight puts your cat at risk for many of the same chronic health problems that an overweight human suffers, including hypertension, diabetes, heart disease, osteoarthritis, and cancer. If your cat's dull coat is due to obesity, the first step is to address the problem. Begin by seeing your veterinarian, who can help you come up with a balanced, low-calorie diet for your cat. I advise you to not attempt this on your own. Your veterinarian can help you determine your cat's daily calorie intake and propose a weight-loss plan. Cats must shed weight in a controlled and steady manner. In an overweight cat, excessive weight loss can lead to hepatic lipidosis, a dangerous liver illness. It took a long time for your cat to gain that weight, and it will take even longer to lose it.

TIP: The quickest way to judge the shape of your cat's figure is to stand over your cat and look down at his body while he is standing, you should be able to see a slight indentation just behind the rib cage. This is an excellent sign that your cat's weight is being maintained at a healthy level. If you can't see any hips, your cat is probably getting a little too heavy. If your British Shorthair is more of a chowhound than a finicky feline, switching to a lower-calorie food rather than reducing the amount could be the answer to weight problems and prevent your cat from turning into Mr. Grumpy Gills. Mainly because obesity problems can lead to conditions such as diabetes, heart problems, and joint diseases. Cats are excellent beggars. Use your willpower and resist the kitty eyes. That devastated look that we have all fallen for is not at all what it seems.

Your Cat's Age

Cats can become less flexible or arthritic as they age, they simply find it hard to twist and turn like they used to. As a result, your feline's coat may become dull and ragged due to age or pain. Brushing your elderly cat more frequently can be your senior cat's ticket back to a soft, luxurious coat. Use a fine-toothed comb to dig down and catch the dead hairs that a brush may miss. If your vet approves, you can also try increasing the omega-3s in your cat's food.

Bathing Too Frequently

Some people bathe their cats to control dander or repel fleas. Frequent baths, however, may become the source of your cat's unkempt coat as frequent washing can lead to dry skin. Bathing your cat is necessary only when their coat is extremely dirty and must be done with a cat-specific shampoo and conditioning rinse. If you've been bathing your cat to relieve your allergy to cat dander, you're not doing yourself or your cat any favours. Bathing has a temporary effect on dander that only lasts a few days. Washing your hands frequently, taking allergy medication, and cleaning the house frequently are all better options. Similarly, the best way to prevent flea is by using flea medication for cats. Never use dog flea products on your cat; they can be fatal.

These are just a few of the causes of dry skin and a dull coat in your cat. Diabetes, parasites, skin infections, allergies, autoimmune diseases, dry winter air, and other issues can also contribute to this problem. If you are concerned about your cat always have it checked by a veterinarian to figure out what's causing your cat's skin or fur problems. Cats are excellent at taking care of themselves in a variety of ways. But they still require our assistance to be happy and healthy.

Healthy Treats

When it come sot your British Shorthair, you can never give them too much attention, but you can give them too many treats. Cats, like humans, can develop weight problems. An estimated 57 percent of cats are overweight or obese, according to a study published by the Association for Pet Obesity Prevention.[5] But can cat treats ever be beneficial to your cat? Are some treats superior to others? It's fine to give your cat treats, however, moderation is essential.[6] How small should it be? Many experts recommend that cat treats account for no more than 5-10% of a cat's total calorie intake as treats add nothing but calories to a cat's diet. The remaining 90% of your cat's calories should come from high-quality, nutrient-dense cat food. It can be difficult to figure out what is in packaged cat treats[7]. This is due to the fact that not all nutrients are listed on food labels, and no calorie count is usually provided so natural treats are usually a better alternative.

Things To Keep In Mind When Treating Cats

Cats, like humans, can develop a taste for treats and may choose to avoid their own food in favor of the treats they enjoy so it's recommended to offering treats no more than two or three times per week. It's also worth noting that good cat foods are formulated to contain the vitamins, minerals, and amino acids that a cat requires for good health, so human food should be limited to a small portion of your cat's diet. We may enjoy raisins, grapes, onions, alcohol, chocolate, salt, and tea, but these and other common foods can be toxic to cats. If you are unsure whether a treat is safe, see Appendix B and if in doubt consult your veterinarian before giving it to your cat. I would also discourage begging by avoiding giving your cat a treat at the dinner table or at the cat's request which could be embarrassing for you or your visitors. In my opinion treats are great for training and exercise. Use cat treats to train your cat in agility exercises or tricks to help them exercise their brain and body. This is especially enjoyable for house cats like the British Shorthair. You can also try rewarding your cat with treats after performing an unpleasant task, such as claw trimming, tooth brushing, or administering medication. Along with verbal praise and petting, this can help to calm a feline who has been forced to do something unpleasant.

You might also have heard of catnip. Catnip is low in calories, so it's an ideal cat treat. Catnip and cat grass, a cereal plant comparable to wheat or oats, are both popular among cats. Both are easy to grow in a sunny window, and pet retailers sell both dried and fresh. Make sure the plant you're giving your cat is cat-safe and don't worry if your British Shorthair regurgitates the cat grass you bought, some cats do, use catnip instead. If you are unsure whether a plant is safe for your cat, consult Appendix A or the ASPCA's website for information on plants toxic to cats. If you suspect your cat has eaten a poisonous plant, contact your vet immediately or the Animal Poison Control Center (USA). As a cat parent you'll know exactly what's in the treats your cat is eating if you cook up small bits of liver or fish for them. You can even make organic cat treats for your cat by purchasing certified organic meat and fish. However, keep in mind that these treats should only make up a small portion of your cat's overall diet[8].

Healthy Cat Treats To Consider

A healthy diet and high-quality snacks can help a cat live a long and healthy life. Because cats can consume treats at any time of day, a proper, healthy treat is just as important as the main meals you provide. Cat treats with nutritional value come in a variety of flavors and styles. Some treats even aid in the prevention of certain health issues, such as hairballs and disease, while others promote general feline well-being. The specific treats you select should be determined by the health benefits you wish to promote for your cat, the feline's tastes and preferences, and your overall budget. A word of caution: treats can cause diarrhea as your British Shorthair kitten may not be used to them so be very careful and take your time when giving your cat treats. I've found that natural treats tend to work best and don't give them tummy issues. My cats like frozen peas, cooked fish, small portions of cheese, and even bananas.

What To Do If Your Cat Is Not Eating

People make fun of cats and their picky eating habits, but in reality, finicky eaters are made and not born. Loss of appetite in cats is typically a sign of disease, my advice is to contact you vet as soon as you notice a change in your cat's feeding habits. One of the most telling signs that something is wrong is a loss of appetite. So, if your cat suddenly stops eating, pay close attention. Infections, kidney failure, pancreatitis, intestinal problems, and cancer are just a few of the possibilities. But it isn't always serious; a dirty bowl or toothache, for example, could cause your cat to stop nibbling. Did you notice your cat's appetite loss shortly after taking it to the vet for routine vaccinations? If this is the case, your cat's refusal to eat could be due to an adverse reaction to the shots. Another thing to consider is that cats are creatures of habit. As a result, a change in routine can cause a loss of appetite. Furthermore, they could also get motion sickness when traveling by car or plane, which can cause nausea and refusal to eat.

Anxiety or depression may also be the cause of your cat's refusal to eat. Changes in the household can sometimes be upsetting to sensitive cats, and new people or changes in familiar schedules can also impact a cat's emotional well-being. Remember that cats, in general, take a long time to adjust to new types of food, so a recent diet change could also be the main cause.

When illness is not the cause, there are some things you can try to get your cat to eat. You may discoverer that certain foods, such as liver or canned tuna, can stimulate the appetite of some cats but remember to only serve these foods in small quantities. Heating the wet food or adding fish oil or broth (without onions or garlic) can also assist with solving eating problems. If your cat has been eating only human food, you can gradually change their diet by combining the people's food with cat food over several weeks. You should be able to slowly adjusting the ratio until your pet is only eating cat food.

Regular, routine feeding times prepare your cat's body for the food it will receive.

A change in eating habits can be a sign of illness. When cats eat regularly, they develop a strong habit. At a glance, it is easy to see if all of the food from a meal has been consumed. If food is left, whether it is all or part of a meal, it might indicate that something is wrong, and it is time to schedule a veterinary call.

Diet FAQs

I was told that kittens should eat as much as they want three or four times per day. Is this correct?

Ad libitum or free-choice feeding refers to feeding a kitten everything it can eat at once. This is not recommended because it can lead to juvenile obesity, binge eating and set the stage for some orthopedic issues and diabetes. Overeating at a single meal can also cause stomach discomfort and bloating, resulting in slower digestion. Cats have been shown to have a genetically determined set point for adult size. Slower, more controlled growth in kittens optimizes adult body condition. Follow your vet or breeder's advice when comes to feeding your British Shorthair.

How many meals should my cat consume per day?

The number of meals a cat consumes per day is entirely dependent on the family's schedule. Cats should eat at least two meals per day, ideally spaced approximately 12 hours apart. However, a breakfast, lunch, afternoon, dinner, and right before bedtime schedule is also an excellent option. Your British Shorthair's needs rise with activity and cold weather, then fall as they get older. Senior cats benefit from better quality, easier-to-digest protein and from increased levels of vitamins and minerals. Antioxidants help to prevent tissue damage, which is more common in elderly cats[9].

My cat does not eat her food all at once. She appears to prefer to graze. What am I supposed to do?

Some cats can actually control their food intake quite well. It is still a good idea to instill a sense of routine around mealtimes. This will make it easier if you decide to add another pet to your family in the future. Simply measure out the entire day's worth of food in the morning and offer the bowl several times throughout the day for grazers. Choose regular times to establish the routine we know is beneficial. The important thing is to use a measured portion for the day, either with a measuring cup or a kitchen scale. Another factor to consider is the use of food toys. There are numerous options available, ranging from rolling food toys that intermittently drop out a kibble of food to stationary food toys that require the cat to work for the food. Your breeder or veterinarian are still the best source of nutritional advice for your cat, answering important questions like what type of food to feed, how much to feed, and how often to feed. Feeding time can be an important time for bonding. Routine and regular feeding times add fun to everyday activities.

CHAPTER 8

DEALING WITH BEHAVIOR PROBLEMS

Do not to confuse behavioral issues with health problems. Feline lower urinary tract disease (FLUTD), for example, causes cats to urinate outside their litter boxes on a regular basis. Prescription drugs might also cause behavioural adverse effects. Consider the anti-inflammatory prednisone, fo example. You will find increased water consumption and, as a result, higher urine production among possible side effects. Ask your vet about the negative effects of any drug provided for your pet. Another thing to consider is that rewarded behaviours are more likely to occur than unrewarded ones. Your cat must not train you. If they tap your head for food at 3 AM and you give in they will surely be back for more the next day. My advice is to give them their meal in the evening so they can spend the night with a full tummy. Leaving dry food available throughout the night can also help with this.

Avoiding The Litter Box

British Shortahirs are clean creatures, and nowhere is this more obvious than in their litter box habits. When your cat refuses to use the litter box – and at least 10% of all cats do – the cause could be anything from an unclean box to an illness. Before you try some simple methods to get them back in the litter box, have them examined by a veterinarian to rule out any health issues. If you've recently adopted a new cat, make sure the litter box is as cat-friendly as possible to avoid future problems. Cats refuse to use the litter box for a variety of reasons.

These common litter box issues may be discouraging your cat,

- A filthy litter box.
- There aren't enough litter boxes for the cats in the house. Some cats don't like sharing it.

- A small litter box.
- A litter box that has a hood or a liner.
- A litter box with raised sides.
- There is too much/little litter in the box.
- Uncomfortable surroundings with limited privacy and multiple escape routes.
- Changes in the type of litter you use.
- Negative connotations Your cat could have been upset while using the litter box. Even if their health has returned to normal, they may associate the box with painful elimination.
- Environmental change such as moving, adding new animals or family members to the household.
- A squabble with another cat in the house.
- A new preference for eliminating particular surfaces or textures such as carpet, potting soil, or bedding.
- Health issues. Your cat could be suffering from a medical condition that makes urinating painful, whether in or out of the litter box.

The following are some common medical conditions that may have an impact on litter box use:

Infection of the urinary tract (UTI). Your cat frequently uses the litter box but only produces small amounts of urine. In that case, he or she may have a urinary tract infection (UTI).

Interstitial cystitis. Feline interstitial cystitis is a complicated disease that causes bladder inflammation. Because of the need to urinate, a cat may eliminate outside the litter box.

Bladder stones or obstruction. Your cat may use the litter box frequently if they have bladder stones or a blockage. They may endure pain, meow, or cry when attempting to eliminate. It's possible that their abdomen is sensitive to touch.

If health issues is not the problem you can implement changes to try and get your cat to use the litter box again:

- Ensure your cat's litter box is clean.
- Once a week, thoroughly rinse the box with baking soda or unscented soap.
- Reduce your use of litter. Cats usually prefer a shallow litter bed that is no more than two inches deep.
- Make use of a larger litter box.
- Use clumping, unscented litter with a medium to fine texture, or the litter they used when they were a kitten. Put a few clean boxes side by

side, each with a different type of litter, and see which one your cat prefers.

- Use no box liners or lids.
- Consider using a self-cleaning litter box, which is generally cleaner than a traditional litter box.
- Place the litter box in a quiet, low-light area where your cat can see anyone approaching and flee quickly. The litter box should be placed away from the food and water dishes.
- Add a few litter boxes in various locations, each with multiple escape routes. Make certain that no children or other animals have access to the boxes.
- If your cat is elderly or has arthritis, use a litter box with low sides so they can easily climb in.
- Give each of your cats a litter box, plus one extra. Place a box on each level if you live in a multi-story building.

You can also ask your veterinarian for fluorescein if you have numerous cats and can't figure out which one isn't using the litter box. Under ultraviolet light, this harmless dye causes urine to shine blue for 24 hours. You'll need to shine a UV light into the litter box to see which cat is using it. Each cat must be fed the dye one at a time (typically in food). An easier approach would be to temporarily confining your cats, one at a time, with a litter box nearby to figure out which cat isn't utilising the litter box. This should only be done for a few days, and you should try to do it in a room without a carpet or a laundry pile. Block off the bathtub or keep an inch of water in it if you're using the bathroom to keep kitten from using it to eliminate.

As deterrent you can also make the surface or location less appealing if your cat has developed a preference for eliminating there. To discourage your cat, you can spray diluted peppermint oil, add bright lights or motion sensors to the area, place tin foil, upside-down carpet runners, or double-sided sticky tape on the preferred surface. If your cat still avoiding the litter box despite your efforts to make it as cat-friendly as possible, the next step should be to consult with an animal behaviorist or your vet.

What Not To Do

It's important to note that pet training is all about patience, not punishment.

- Do not rub their noses in urine or feces.
- Do not chastise them or drag them to the litter box.
- Do not confine them to a small room with a litter box before attempting other methods to solve their elimination problem.

- Do not place the litter box close to their food and water.
- Do not bribe them with treats to get them to use the litter box. Cats prefer not to be disturbed while eliminating.

To help them overcome their aversion to the box, you can place toys and treats near it. Also, instead of an ammonia-based cleanser, use an enzymatic cleanser or bicarb to clean up spills. Then, cover the area with foil or plastic sheeting and seal it off for a few weeks to allow the neutralizer to do its job.

How To Discourage Night-Time Madness

Cats have a different sleep-wake cycle than other animals, and they are often awake late at night. This is due to the fact that cats are crepuscular, meaning they hunt and are active in the evenings and early mornings. Your cat may exhibit a variety of behaviors that keep you awake at night. Wild playing, toes nibbling and pouncing, purring in your ear, walking across your back, weeping or yowling are all behaviors, which may begin in the evening or awaken you in the middle of the night. To prevent this it's better for your British Shorthair to have their own sleeping place in the house. Another thing to consider is that if you leave your cat at home alone during the day while you are at work or school your cat may spend the majority of the day sleeping or relaxing during this time. All that snoozing during the day can result in a hyperactive cat at night. They may also become bored and seek more interaction and attention. British Shortahirs are social pets, so your cat may have extra energy or may be waking you up to get your attention. Lack of night time nibbles might also keep your cat awake in the middle of the night, it's a good idea to have some dry food available during this time. Sleeping patterns in cats frequently change as they get older. You may notice that your cat is more active at night, which can be caused by health issues as part of the natural aging process. Speaking of health issues, certain conditions such as pain, anxiety, hyperthyroidism, persistent illness and dementia may also cause your cat to be hyperactive, uneasy, vocal, or needy at night. With a few tweaks during the day, you can train your cat to sleep at night. The most important part is to not reward your cat's nighttime behavior with attention but rather to schedule daytime play with your cat. Play will keep your cat awake. Spend time with your cat after work or in the evening. Allowing catnaps while playing with or training your cat should be discouraged. Rescheduling evening meals may also make your cat sleepy before bed. Set an automatic feeder for early morning feeding if your cat has a habit of waking up early for food. Allowing feedings in the middle of the night, on the other hand, will teach your cat to stay awake for food. You can also set up a comfortable sleeping area with a litter box as far away from your bedroom as possible. Place a towel at the bottom of the door to prevent scratching or rattling. Medications might be helpful. If nothing else works, your vet may recommend prescription or natural sleep aids like melatonin or valerian. Your cat, on the other hand, may develop a resistance to sleeping pills. After a few nights, they may no longer be effective.

How To Discourage Urine Marking

One of the most common issues people have with their feline companions is inappropriate peeing. This is predominantly experienced by owners of unneutered males. It can happen for a variety of reasons. Kidney problems and arthritis, for example, can cause your cat to urinate in the wrong place. If these issues have been ruled out, the cause is likely to be behavioral. Smells are a common way for animals to communicate. Cats are territorial and have different ways to manage their territory. Cats are not well equipped to deal with conflict. When there is a confrontation or a change, they may become stressed. Spraying, or urine marking, is their non-verbal way of telling other cats or new people to back off. Your cat may also be spraying to express themselves about territory. Feline urine marking may occur as a result of your cat feeling threatened, stressed or having a a strong desire to mate. The main reason your British Shorthair would spray is simply because he has not been neutered and want to mark his territory. In decades of owning cats and breeding them I have never heard of spraying problems among neutered boys. They spray because of the hormones they produce, unneutered cats have a higher proclivity to mark. Although neutering reduces odor and motivation to spray, feline urine marking occurs in up to 10% of neutered cats. Conflict with outdoor cats can also lead to spraying. When an indoor cat sees an outdoor cat, he or she may become distressed. If the outdoor cat starts spraying nearby, they may become even more agitated. If this occurs, your cat may begin to spray inside the house to mark its territory. If this is the case, close the curtains or block any view of the outdoor cat that your cat may have. Using a pheromone diffuser will assist your cat in relaxing and reducing anxiety. Try talking to the cat's owner's neighbor or installing sound-emitting remote deterrents. In order to be able to tell the difference between a litter box issue and feline urine marking, look for the following signs:

- A spraying cat will have its tail straight up in the air and project its backside toward the target. The tail may quiver or shake.
- A spraying cat will usually only mark with urine and will still use the litter box regularly. It is unusual for a cat to mark with stool.
- A cat with a litter box issue will urinate on the floor or another horizontal surface. A spraying cat will usually leave their urine on a vertical surface, such as a wall.

Urine Marking In A Home With More Than One Cat

Cats are averse to change. Anything from a guest to a new infant can upset them. Also, when a new pet is brought into the house, they can become agitated. The conflict between cats frequently goes unnoticed by cat owners because it manifests itself in subtle ways before escalating. Cat conflict styles can be classified as passive-aggressive. They may silently stare at each other or block each other from litter boxes and food dishes before spraying, hissing, and fighting. In multi-cat households, it is critical to first ensure that cat spraying or soiling is not occurring due to another cat bullying and denying them access to the litter box. Separating cats may be necessary to determine who the perpetrator is. You can prevent conflict by organizing their environment so that all pets have easy access to what they require and avoid other behavioral issues. It may be necessary to distribute resources such as food, water, and litter boxes throughout the house to ensure that each cat has access to them. Make sure to have one litter box for each cat, as well as an extra one.

- Provide different perching areas for your cats, each with room for only one cat.
- You may need to separate your cats by making separate areas for them. Closed doors and baby gates can be useful.
- Make time to play and cuddle with each of your cats so that they all feel loved equally.
- Using a pheromone diffuser can help to reduce anxiety. These can be found at our website, www.muffinandpoppy.co.uk or pet stores.

Male and female cats can both spray. Saying that I have never come across spraying females. Male cats who have not been neutered are the most likely to do so. They also have the most potently odorous urine.

What Should You Do If Your Cat Sprays

The appropriate response to spraying can help deter your cat from spraying again. When your cat sprays, do the following:

- Use a mild-fragrance soap or bicarb to clean soiled areas. Strong-smelling cleaners may cause your cat to spray again.
- Inaccessible soiled areas should be made inaccessible. This will prevent your cat from marking the same area in the future.
- To discourage spraying, keep items that smell foreign to your cat out of reach.

CHAPTER 9

CARING GUIDELINES FOR YOUR CAT

Nothing beats a little pampering to make your British Shortair feel and look like the star that they are. Like all felines your British Shorthair is a compulsive groomer. You've probably seen these Brad Pitt and Angelina Jolies of the cat world give themselves a bath daily. However, as tidy as they are generally, they may require a little assistance from time to time to feel or look their best. Grooming your cat should be enjoyable for both you and them. Try to schedule a grooming session for after dinner, when your cat is already calm and sleepy. You should also be in a good mood — your cat will notice if you're upset or stressed during the grooming session, which can stress them out. The first few times you groom your cat, he or she may become impatient with all the attention so keep your first few sessions to no more than five minutes. Once your British Shortahir has become accustomed to the routine, you can gradually increase the amount of time you spend cleaning them. This is also a good time to get your cat used to being handled. Play with anything from their ears to their feet to make them feel less stressed. It's very important not to force your cat to accept grooming. Take a break and try again later if your cat appears upset or stressed. If you need to bathe your cat, enlist the assistance of another person to help you. If your cat behaves well during grooming, never be afraid to praise or reward them.

Brushing

Your British Shorthair is low maintenance when comes to their plush coat and, usually, only require brushing once a week. Brushing them will keep their lush thick fur looking more gorgeous than any Louis Vuitton coat. Brushing removes dirt and tangles while also spreading healthy oils throughout their coat, keeping their skin and fur healthy and removing irritation.

For *shorthair cats* start at their head and work your way down to their tail with a metal comb to loosen dead fur, then repeat the process with a bristle or rubber brush to remove the dead hair. Always exercise caution when approaching your cat's face, belly, or chest.

Long-haired cats require a little more attention and should be brushed daily. Make sure you brush under the arm pits and belly as they seem to get tangled up more easily. Begin with your cat's legs and belly and work your way up. Brush the fur in an upward motion to assist in lifting and cleaning it. If necessary, part the fur on your cat's tail down the middle and brush each side separately.

Teeth Brushing

Dental hygiene helps to keep your cat healthy. This may not be your favourite thing to do but daily brushing will ensure that your cat's mouth stays as disease free as possible. You can start with a finger brush or a small, soft bristle brush and feline toothpaste. The best time to start is as soon as your kitten has permanent teeth, at around 6 months. If you have an adult cat it will take more patience and determination but it can be done.

Bathing

You'll be able to tell if your cat requires a bath. They will either be oily to the touch or will have come into contact with something smelly or sticky. In these cases, you'll need to get a cat-specific shampoo (pH 7.5) and give your cat a proper bath. Never use shampoo for humans as cats have different pH balance than humans shampoo (pH5.5).

1. Brush your cat as much as possible to prevent hair from clogging your drain.
2. Gather all you need such as cat shampoo, sponge, face towel, towel and place a rubber mat in your bathtub or sink so your cat can stand up comfortably.
3. Fill a few inches of warm, not hot, water in the sink or tub. Four to six inches (10-15cm) should be enough.
4. Get your cat completely wet with a plastic jug or mug or a gentle spray hose. Use the sponge or face towel to clean their face and head area. Do not let water enter your kitten's ears.
5. Apply a small amount of shampoo, working your way from the neck to the tail.
6. Rinse off all of the shampoo, being careful not to get it in their eyes. Don't forget to rinse under the armpit and tail area really well.
7. Apply conditioner if required.
8. Use your hand to remove the excess of water from your cat and dry

your cat off with a warm, dry towel and keep them warm for the rest of the day.

Taking Care Of Fleas

Fleas are most common during summer and can be caught from other animals, the outdoors, or from your home if they've been brought in on shoes or clothes. A cat who frequently scratches, chews their skin, or appears restless could be infested with fleas. You can relieve their itching (and protect yourself) by learning how to detect and eliminate fleas on your pet and in your home. Before resorting to flea treatments, I would advise you to check to see if these pests have taken up residence on your cat.

- Keep an eye out for any movement in their fur. It's time to fight fleas if you see tiny bugs bouncing off their coat.
- Are there tiny dark dots (flea faeces) under the fur close to the skin?
- Using a fine-toothed metal flea comb, comb your cat from head to tail several times per day. This will remove adult fleas and their eggs while also relieving itching.
- Then, to kill the fleas, dip the comb in a solution of warm to hot water and liquid dish detergent.

A flea's dream home is your cat's warm, furry coat and nourishing blood supply. Protect your pet with a flea barrier to keep these pesky pests at bay. Spot-on treatments are more effective, safer and convenient than traditional dust, shampoos, and sprays. You can get them from your veterinarian or online. Inquire with your vet about where to apply the product to your cat, how much to apply, and how often to use it. If you are not receiving the treatment from your veterinarian, read the product label first to ensure that it is safe for cats. The most common active ingredients and brands are:

- Fipronil is a type of pesticide (Frontline Plus)
- Imidacloprid is a pesticide (Advantage, Advocate)
- Selamectin (Stronghold/Revolution) is a type of insecticide.
- Fluralaner is a type of fluralaner (Bravecto)
- A flea collar containing flumethrin and imidacloprid (Seresto) can also be effective.

Adult fleas on your cat are killed in 30 minutes by the pill nitenpyram (Capstar). However, it has no long-term effects. Spinosad (Comfortis) is a quick-acting chewable that kills fleas before they lay eggs. It offers a full month of flea protection to aid in the prevention of future hatchings. Natural options include CedarCide and Pet Protector safe tag.

A WORD OF CAUTION: never put a dog flea treatment or a household flea spray on a cat. They often contain permethrin, which is extremely poisonous to cats (as well as fish and birds). Contact your vet immediately if your cat has come into contact with a dog flea treatment, or household flea spray.

How To Get Rid Of Fleas In Your Home

In a single day, a female flea can lay up to 50 eggs. These glide off your cat and onto your carpet, couch, or blanket with ease. Allow them to hatch, and you'll be dealing with a full-fledged flea infestation. A thorough cleaning of your home can assist you in resolving the issue. Vacuum and clean the carpets, cushions, and cracks, and crevices in the floor to remove any eggs before they hatch. This method will also get rid of live fleas. Just remember to dispose of the vacuum bag or wash out the canister with warm, soapy water when you're finished. Then, remove any bedding, sofa covers, or other fabrics that your pet has touched and place them in the washing machine. Use hot water to ensure that no bugs survive the wash cycle.

Fleas that persist despite treatment may necessitate more drastic measures. You may need to remove all pets and family members from the house, and then use a flea spray to coat carpets and other surfaces. The most effective sprays contain methoprene or pyriproxyfen. If you're concerned about the presence of chemicals in your home, try a natural citrus spray. Pets, children, and others should be kept away until all surfaces have dried. Remember to treat all your pets as any untreated pet can be a flea reservoir, and you'll never be able to control the flea problem. Fleas will win the battle until all of your pets are treated.

Taking Care Of Your Cat's Ears

Cleaning can be done with a soft cloth and lukewarm water. Home made remedies include Witch Hazel, 50:50 solution of organic apple cider vinegar and purified water. Your vet will also be able to advise on this. Cats don't get ear infections very often, but the cause can be complicated when they do. If your vet has ruled out ear mites, which are responsible for roughly half of all feline ear infections, in that case, further investigation will be necessary to find out what's causing your cat's outer or middle ear infection. It could be caused by allergies, a mass, or something lodged in the ear canal. The condition is first diagnosed by looking into the ear canal with an instrument known as an otoscope. The ear debris is then examined under a microscope to see if it contains yeast, bacteria, or ear mites. Further testing may need sedation or

X-rays, but treating ear infections is usually straightforward. The most commonly used treatments are antibiotics, antiparasitics, antifungals, and corticosteroids. What is critical is that you take your cat to the vet as soon as you notice signs of ear discomfort. Chronic ear infections can cause deafness and facial paralysis.

Ear Infections

Ear infections are usually a secondary condition unless your cat has picked up mites from another animal. That is, they are the result of another underlying medical problem. Some of the contributing causes and perpetuating factors for external ear infections, known as otitis externa, and middle ear infections, known as otitis media, are:

- Wax buildup in the ear canal
- Overgrowth of yeast or bacteria or both
- Thick hair in the ear canal
- Allergies to foods or pollen
- Autoimmuny diseases
- Tumors and polyps in the ear canal
- Eardrum rupture
- Inadequate ear cleaning
- Foreign body such as bristle from lawn.
- Irritating substances in the environment
- Diabetes mellitus.

Infections of the middle ear are typically the result of an infection spread from the outer ear canal to the middle ear.

Symptoms Of An Ear Infection

A cat's discomfort is manifested by scratching or pawing at its ear, as well as shaking or tilting its head in the direction of the painful ear. Other symptoms to look out for are: yellow or black discharge, ear flap or ear canal redness or swelling, wax accumulation on or near the ear canal, ear discharge that resembles coffee grounds (a symptom of ear mites), bad odor, hearing impairment and disorientation or loss of balance.

Treating Ear Infections

If your cat has ear mites or a yeast or bacterial infection, your veterinarian will treat it with anti-parasitics, antifungals, or antibiotics, as needed. These remedies come in the form of ointment or eardrops. If the eardrum is healthy but the infection has migrated to the middle ear, your veterinarian may prescribe antibiotics, either oral or injectable. To start treatment, your veterinarian may cut the fur surrounding the cat's ear canal to make cleaning and drying easier. If the inside of the ear flap is pink and the canal is clear, you can continue to inspect your cat's ear at home. If ear drops are recommended, gently lift the ear flap and squeeze the solution into the ear canal. Massage the base of the ear gently to help the medicine enter the ear canal. If the problem is chronic a medication to help reduce swelling of the tissue in the ear canal may be prescribed. Surgery is sometimes required to remove swollen tissue that has narrowed or closed the ear canal. Ear infections are more common in cats who have diabetes, allergies, or a weakened immune system.

Regularly inspecting the ear for redness, debris, or odour is the best approach to avoid a painful ear infection. Ears that are healthy are pale pink in colour, have no visible debris or odour, and have little to no ear wax. You can spot a probable ear infection early and treat it before it progresses by checking the ears on a regular basis. The veterinarian should either show you how to clean your cat's ear or clean it for you. Never put a cleaning equipment in your cat's ear canal unless your veterinarian tells you to.

Taking Care Of Your Cat's Eyes

Cats should have their eyes gently wiped with a warm, damp cloth to remove any build up of daily secretions in the corner of their eyes. The coating on your cat's eyes is very important in keeping them healthy. This layer, known as the tear film, removes debris. It keeps their eyes moist and nourishes them. It is also effective against bacteria. Watery discharge is sometimes a sign that your cat's eyes are in full fight mode against a threat to their health. The majority of the time, the cause is minor and will resolve on its own.

If you notice that the tissues around one or both eyes are inflamed and red, as well as a watery discharge, they most likely have conjunctivitis, also called pinkeye. It is the most common type of eye problem in cats. It can be caused by an infection, an allergy, or even dust. Because pinkeye is contagious, most cats will get it at some point in their lives. It can affect animals of any age, but it primarily affects young animals. Pinkeye is also caused by the feline herpes virus. Your cat can be immunized against this, but they could have contracted it as a kitten. They are infected for life if they have the virus. However, the vaccine can help to alleviate their symptoms. Reducing stress can help to prevent flare-ups. Pinkeye usually goes away on its own. However, talk to your vet if you notice anything unusual and if your cat appears to be in pain.

If the discharge is yellow or sticky lab tests can assist your veterinarian in determining the source of the problem. Clear mucus indicates that your cat is infected with a virus. The vet will probably tell you to wait a week or two and see if it clears up on its own. In most cases it will. A bacterial infection is indicated by green or yellow mucus. You'll most likely be given antibiotic eyedrops or ointment to treat it.

Allergies

Cats are allergic to the same things that humans are such as pollen, mold, mildew, dust, medicine , flea-repelling products, perfumes and cleaning supplies. Your veterinarian can determine whether or not your cat has an allergy and recommend the best treatment options.

The British Shorthair Susceptibility To Tearing

The British Shortahir breed have short, rounded faces and skulls. This may result in a lot of tears which can be cleaned with soft tissue or clean cloth. Tears that stream down their cheeks may also stain their hair. There are various products available to treat these stains, but some may contain ingredients that are not safe. Inquire with your vet about which one to use. I use soft tissues to clean my cat's eyes and it seems to work fine, it seems that with time the more you dry their eyes the less teary they get.

Claw Clipping

Cat's claws are something we don't think about until we notice they're too long. If you only touch your cat's feet when it's time to trim their nails, your cat may be bothered by the unusual experience. Play with your cat's feet when you're not about to trim their nails to make things easier. This allows them to become accustomed to the sensation and feel safe. It also doesn't hurt to praise your cat and lavish them with treats while playing with their toes. After a few weeks, your cat will most likely accept nail trimmings calmly. Here's what to do:

- To begin, gently squeeze the top and bottom of your cat's foot until their claws appear.
- Only cut the white tip of your cat's nails with a dedicated cat nail trimmer.
- Never cut your cat's nail in the inner pink area (called quick) as it contains nerves and blood vessels.
- Keep styptic powder on hand in case you accidentally cut the quick. The styptic powder will quickly stop the bleeding.

Although the British Shorthair is not known for excessive scratching, it's important to get your cat used to regular nail clipping from an early age. Cutting your cat's nails can be a stressful experience for everyone involved, but it doesn't have to be. Any cat can be educated to tolerate and even love having its nails cut, according to cat behaviourists. Following a few basic suggestions might help you and your cat relax when getting their nails done on a regular basis.

The best way to start is by training your cat to accept nail trimming when he or she is a kitten. This should always be done in a calm, quiet environment, regardless of when you begin. Trim your cat's claws ideally when they are sleepy, such as after a meal. Keep your distance from windows and other pets that could distract you or them. Bring your cat somewhere where you can comfortably sit with them in your lap. Remember that the British Shorthair is a less restraint cat. Put your pet on your lap and pick up one paw at a time. If you cat won't stay still you can wrap the rascal in a thick towel, that will hopefully comfort them and try to clip their claws again. If that fails or they try to bite because they get grumpy use an astronaut helmet. I've found that the best way to achieve claw clipping success is by asking someone to hold my cat in their lap as they hold their heads away from the procedure while stroking it under the chin with plenty of words of affirmation. That provides the distraction they need for me to quickly clip their claws. Some cats dislike having their feet played with more than they dislike having their claws trimmed. Taking the time to get them used to having their paws touched will pay dividends in the long run.

Hold one paw between your fingers and gently rub it for three seconds. If your cat moves during the process, gently mimic their movement. Then squeeze the paw so that one of the claws extends. Give your cat a treat and immediately release it. If possible, repeat this two or three times per day until your cat becomes accustomed to it and does not appear to resist as much. You may find that the dew claw on the side is difficult to reach. If your pet gets fidgety, let him down and finish the job later.

Getting Used To The Clipper Monster

Unfamiliar objects can be frightening to your cat, so leave the clippers out for your cat to see it. You can even place a treat on them to entice your cat to sniff them and become acquainted with the offending device. Some cats can be terrified by the evil sound made by the clipper when trimming takes place. Place a piece of dry spaghetti in the clippers while your cat is on your lap. Hold the clippers close to their paws and gently massage one paw before cutting the noodle, so it makes a cracking noise. Give your cat a treat right away for accepting the noise and the massage. After you've spent some time acclimating your cat to the idea, it's time to get busy with the clipping. Place your cat in your lap with its back to you. Take one of your cat's paws in your hand and gently press the pad until you can clearly see their claw. If the claw needs to be trimmed, only cut the sharp point and avoid the quick. When you've finished trimming the nail, immediately release the paw and reward your cat if they've noticed what you're doing. If your cat is calm and doesn't seem to mind the trimming, proceed to the next nail. Your British Shorthair might complain after you have trimmed two or three of their nails. Stop and let them go if this happens. Always give your cat a treat and words of affirmation after a trim. This demonstrates to your cat that trimming is not stressful and results in enjoyable times. To get all of their nails trimmed, you may need to schedule several short sessions. It's important to trim only the white part of the claw. To do this look carefully at the cat's nail, you will see that the curved tips are translucent to white. The base of the claw, the quick, is an extremely vascular region. Be very careful not to catch this area when you are clipping your cat's claws. As you gain experience, you will be able to work more quickly and confidently. The faster you move through the claw clipping procedure and the more lightly you hold your cat, the better for you both. Another piece of advice is to not use nail clippers intended for humans; instead, purchase a pair of small animal clippers with grips like pliers. They will give you better control. If you are in any way nervous about doing this, it would be a wise precaution to watch a YouTube tutorial or ask your vet to show you how to clip your cat's claws before you try to do it yourself. Most cats' claws should be trimmed every two to three weeks. Getting into a routine will help you keep your cat's nails in check. If you're having trouble trimming their claws, you can seek advice from a groomer or veterinarian.

What Not To Do

- Never attempt to trim your cat's nails if he or she is upset or if you are in a bad mood. This adds to the stress of the situation.
- Never rush through a nail trim. You could nick the quick if you cut too deeply.
- Don't chastise or punish your cat for putting up a fight. This will only encourage them to avoid further trimming.
- Try not to trim all of your cat's nails at once.

Declawing

Please note that declawing your cat is something entirely different to clipping your cat's nails and illegal under the animal cruelty laws. It can result in long-term complications and pain. Instead, provide scratching posts for your cats, consult with your veterinarian about nail covers, or trim their nails more frequently. Do not be surprised if your cat's adoption agreement will expressly forbid declawing your cat in strongly worded terms. This surgery is illegal in Europe and in the United States for the simple reason that it's inhumane and completely unnecessary. To remove the claw, the last digit of the cat's toe must be amputated. The procedure is painful; it affects the animal's mobility for the duration of its life. It takes away the cat's primary means of self-defence. Cats introduced to scratching apparatus early in their life and whose claws are regularly clipped are not destructive. Declawing is a radical measure done exclusively for the convenience of the owner. It is a callous disregard for the welfare of the cat.

CHAPTER 10

Finding A Vet, Medications, Vaccines And Other Essential Details

Since the beginning of time, humans have had a relationship with animals, taking them into their homes and hearts. In many cases, pet owners regard their animals in the same way that they regard their children. Pets, like their human owners, may experience medical emergencies. Because of advancements in veterinary science, owners can now seek out many procedures previously reserved for humans only. These procedures can be costly. Although vet treatment for cats might not be as expensive as dogs, the average cost of an emergency veterinary treatment for cats could range between £250 ($335) and £900 ($1210).

Annual exams and vaccines, blood work, and dental cleanings are all part of primary pet care. However, specialized areas of pet care such as neurology and oncology are experiencing rapid growth. The prospect of high medical costs can deter some prospective pet owners from adopting a pet. Furthermore, for those who do adopt, the possibility of costly procedures and medicines can lead to a decision to euthanize a pet, a practice known as "economic euthanasia." That is why it is very important for your pet to be fully insured. Below is a list of the average cost of the more commonly seen health disorders and injuries seen in cats:

- Open wounds that need veterinary attention £350 ($470).
- Growth or tumour removal £600 ($805).
- Cat bite abscesses £250+ ($335+).
- Hyperthyroidism treatment £350 ($470).
- Cystitis treatment £300 ($402).
- Respiratory disorder £480 ($644).

- Cysts and warts removal £500 ($670).
- Accident treatments. Cats are more at risk of being hit by a car than a dog, The average cost of treating a cat that's been injured in an accident can be in the region of £450+ ($604+). If they were involved in a road traffic accident, this could cost around £900 ($1200).

Finding A Vet

The best way to find a great local vet is to ask others who own cats. If you do not know any cat owner, contact your local animal rescue, pet stores or go online and find an online discussion or Facebook group in your area and start asking for recommendations. Other cat owners can also help you avoid undesirable vets. Ask plenty of questions, such as why do you recommend this particular vet? Is the vet personable and knowledgeable about cats in general? Do they have experience? Are their prices reasonable? Find out as much as you can as to why the person likes the vet. Also, ask them what they do not like about the vet.

Preventative Disease Guidelines

Because cats age faster than humans, they may need to see their doctor more frequently than we do. Cats mature quickly during their first two years of life, so a two-year-old cat is thought to be equivalent to about 25 human years. Following that, one feline year is approximately four human years. A four-year-old cat is approximately 33 years old, and a ten-year-old cat is approximately 57 years old. A discussion of your cat's daily life will provide your veterinarian with an overall picture of their health. Even healthy cats should have a veterinary examination at least once a year. More frequent visits may be required if your cat is older or has medical issues. Changes in your cat's demeanour may occur so gradually that you are unaware of them until you are prompted to do so. Is your cat eating well and having regular bowel movements? Is he straining to urinate? Is he sluggish to get up when he's lying down? Is he ever out of breath, coughing, or sneezing? Is he a heavy drinker? Are there any growths or bumps? Your responses will direct the veterinarian down a diagnostic path that will result in your companion feeling better. Furthermore, in order to prevent parasites in warmer climates or on cats that are allowed outside medication should be given regularly to prevent heartworms and intestinal parasites all year. Many of these medications also work to keep fleas and ticks at bay.

Be aware of all the following signs of potential illness and follow up with a vet should any of these symptoms or behavioral changes appear in your British Shorthair.

Weight change (gain/loss). Cats with a healthy weight have a fat pad over the ribs, but the bones can still be felt through this layer. Looking down at the cat, you should be able to see an indentation behind the rib cage where the 'hips' start. According to studies, leaner cats live longer and have fewer health issues. Your veterinarian will give your cat a body condition score and make dietary and exercise recommendations to help your cat maintain a healthy BMI.

Gait change. Physical changes in the way your cat moves, including a reluctance to perform certain motions like running or jumping, there might be a chance your companion is experiencing joint or muscle pain.

Nose moisture. A dry or runny nose could indicate the presence of a cold or an infection. A cat's nose under normal circumstances should be clean and dry but not cracked. There should be no discharge from the nostrils, either clear or discolored.

Discharge from the eyes. All cats occasionally accumulate 'matter' in the eyes, however, there should never be a running discharge or constant tears. The expression of a British Shorthair should be gentle but engaged. Make sure the pupils are equal and centered and that the whites are not discolored and have only minimal visible blood vessels.

Ear sensitivity and visible debris. Poor hygiene and care can occasionally lead to problems with ear mites and similar irritating parasites. A foul odor emanating from the ear is always a key warning sign. The inner surface of the ear should be clean and smooth in appearance with no visible redness. If the area is inflamed, hot to the touch, and/or black debris is present your cat should be seen by a vet.

Pale gums and yellow teeth. A cat's gums should be pink, and the teeth should be clean and white. Any dark or yellow build-up on the teeth is an indication that plaque is present. Regular dental exams are also critical in detecting any lesions that might indicate the presence of oral cancer. If found early, such growths can be managed with some success. A cat's oral health has an impact on his overall health. Simply put, cats who keep their mouths clean live longer. Bacteria that cause periodontal disease do not stay in the mouth. These organisms enter the bloodstream and travel to major organs such as the kidneys, liver, and heart, where they cause health problems. Cats' teeth may need to be cleaned every 1-2 years. Dental care is extremely important. Some cat owners brush their cat's teeth using feline toothpaste and brushes available at the veterinary clinic. A dental care kit from a vet typically costs about £6 to £12 ($8 to $16). Never use human products for this purpose on a cat. While such a routine may sound absolutely impossible, if started early, cats are often quite amiable about the whole process. Since it's much more a matter of just getting the paste in the cat's mouth, some owners use their index finger as a brush. It's never too late to start looking after your cat's teeth, and it's certainly worth a try to see how your cat will respond to the process.

Immunizations

Vaccines are classified into two types: core vaccines and non-core vaccines (optional vaccines). All cats should be immunized against rabies (if you are not in the UK), feline enteritis, feline herpesvirus 1, and calicivirus (unless they have medical conditions that prevent vaccination), usually in a combined FVRCP vaccination. Cats at risk of exposure should also be immunized against the feline leukemia virus. It's standard practice for kittens to leave to their permanent homes fully vaccinated. This should take place at nine and twelve weeks of age. Having your kitten vaccinated will protect your pet from four of the most serious cat diseases: feline infectious enteritis, feline herpes virus, feline calicivirus and feline leukaemia virus.

All of these diseases are contagious and can be spread by infected cats. Kittens should then have an annual vaccination appointment each year, throughout their lives, in order keep their immunity topped up and maintain protection. Whether you have a kitten or an adult cat, your veterinarian can advise you on which vaccines are best and how frequently your feline should be immunized. It is usually determined by their age, overall health, and way of life. The vet will also consider how long vaccines are supposed to last and how likely it is that your cat will come into contact with a particular disease. In addition, if you're not in the UK, many local and state governments have laws governing vaccines such as rabies.

When should vaccines be administered? Kittens should begin receiving vaccinations when they are 9 to 12 weeks old. They must then be boosted a year later. Adult cats require vaccinations less frequently, usually once a year or every three years, depending on how long a vaccine is designed to last.

Which shots do they require? Some vaccinations are required for all cats. They guard against:

- Rabies (if you are not in the UK)
- Panleukopenia is a type of leukopenia (also known as feline distemper)
- Calicivirus in cats
- Feline viral rhinotracheitis is a contagious respiratory infection caused by a virus.
- The feline viral rhinotracheitis, calicivirus, and panleukopenia vaccinations are frequently combined in a single shot (FVRCP), sometimes referred to as the "distemper shot."

Your cat may require additional shots depending on how much time they spend outside, how often they are exposed to other cats, and the diseases prevalent in your area. They are as follows:

Feline leukemia. This is a severe viral infection that spreads through bodily fluids such as saliva, feces, urine, and milk. The vaccine is advised for kittens and then again 12 months later. The cat's lifestyle will influence future vaccine recommendations. Because feline leukemia cannot be cured, prevention is the top priority.

Bordetella. Cats who go to the groomer or stay at a kennel may be vaccinated against this infection, spreading quickly in areas with a high animal population. The vaccine will not prevent the disease, but it will keep your cat from becoming very ill due to it. While it is no longer routinely recommended for grooming or boarding, individual businesses may require it.

If your cat spends all of its time indoors, you might believe that they are immune to these diseases. They may, however, catch airborne germs that enter through a window or door. Even the most docile cats will occasionally make a break for it. If your cat ventures outside, you must ensure that they are safe. Indoor cats can pick up bacteria and viruses from kennels and from bringing a new cat home. Keep in mind that vaccines do not provide complete immunity to diseases. Limit your pet's contact with infected animals and exposure to environments where diseases may be more prevalent.

Hairballs

The barbs on your cat's tongue remove loose and dead fur as they groom themselves. These strands of hair are swallowed. The majority of hair travels through the digestive tract, however some hair may collect in the stomach and create a hairball. Hairballs are eventually ejected by cats, who vomit them up. Please note that they will not look like a perfect furball like the ones you see on cartoons or movies. Cylinder-shaped hairballs are the most common shape. You could mistake one for poop if you see one on your precious rug. Hairballs are frequently wet and the same size and form as faeces, although the colour may be closer to your cat's food. However, a close examination of a hairball reveals that it is made up of densely packed hair and does not smell like poop. Hairballs are more common in longhaired cats, such as British Longhair, Persians and Maine Coons. Don't automatically attribute all vomiting to innocuous hairballs. Hairballs are the most likely diagnosis if you notice a large hairball in the vomited material, which happens occasionally. However, cats who vomit hairballs on a regular basis could potentially have an underlying disease, which should be investigated by a veterinarian.

Neutering And Sspaying

When you adopt a British Shorthair kitten from a quality breeder, you will be required to agree to have your pet spayed or neutered before twelve months of age. This will cost around £50 - £100 (similar price range in dollars). Spaying or neutering can have a variety of health and behavioral benefits. Surgery can help to prevent infections and some types of cancer. Neutered males will be calmer, less prone to wander and less likely to spray while spayed females will be less agitated, irritable and aggressive towards other cats. These advantages, as well as the timing of your cat's surgery, will be discussed with your veterinarian.

Pregnancy Care

A female cat can reach sexual maturity between four and six months of age and feline pregnancy usually lasts for 63 days. The mother (also called queen) will usually deliver 4-6 kittens (but anything between 1-12 is also possible) and will give birth to two litters evey year. You will need to provide a nice quiet and warm place for her and also increase her food intake. As the kittens get bigger she will also sleep more. Towards the end of pregnancy, about a week before she gives birth, she will start nesting and will need a nice and warm box for her and the kittens. The box must have room enough for her to deliver the kittens to prevent accidents. She will also eat less during this period. Once she gives birth to the first kitten the others should arrive in an interval or approximately 15-20 minutes. Delivery is usually straight forward. There will be blood and mess. The mother might meaw or hiss as she pushes the kittens out, tha's normal. If you have to move the kittens, do so wearing clean or disposable gloves, hygiene is essential during this time. Have clean towels handy and your vet phone ready in case of any questions or concerns.

Identifying Feline Illnesses

Because cats cannot communicate, veterinarians cannot inquire as to how they are feeling or what is bothering them. Furthermore, innate survival instincts cause cats to conceal their illnesses to avoid appearing weak and vulnerable to predators. This means that thorough physical examinations are essential[1]. Furthermore, because your veterinarian cannot see what is going on inside your cat's body, blood and urine tests must complete the health picture. The preventive medicine steps below will help your cat live a longer, healthier life by detecting problems early on when treatment is more successful and less expensive. A healthy neutered or spayed British Shorthair can live to be 14 to 20 years or more and with proper care they may not suffer from the rare issues noted below[2].

Allergies. When cats are suffering from allergies they will typically present itchy skin or earn problems. Other symptoms include obsessive scratching, bitting, licking and chewing at themselves. Cats can develop allergies to dust, chemicals, grass, pollen, mold, cigarette smoke (avoid this at all cost due to asthma risk), flea solutions, cleaning materials and even wool and cotton. Look for symptoms on the stomach, inside of the legs and at the tails or paws.

Allergies are usually seasonal and it will be more severe in the spring or autumn. Airbourne irritants can cause coughing, sneezing and watery eyes. The best thing to do if your cat is exposed to an allergy source is to give them a bath with proper feline shampoo. Food allergies account for only 10% of feline allergies and are usually caused by a low-quality diet. The solution to food allergies is to change your cat's diet to high-quality food. The easier way to diagnose food allergies is by totally removing your cat's usual food and treats, then introducing a free of allergy-causing hydrolyzed protein diet until the symptoms are no longer apparent. This can take up to 12 weeks. Once all symptoms disappear other foods can then be individually introduced to identify which one causes the allergic reaction.

Feline Calici (FCV). This is a highly contagious and easily transmitted virus with various different strains, much like the human flu. This mutant virus can cause loss of appetite, respiratory infections or 'colds', pneumonia, limping and death. The virus is transmitted through the air when a cat sneezes, shared bows and contact with other infected cats.

Feline Infectious Peritonitis (FIP). This disease is caused by a type of coronavirus. It should be stressed that there is no connection between FIP and the human COVID-19. FIP causes damage to the blood vessels (vasculitis) and fluid build-up inside the abdomen or chest. This is a complex, serious, and ultimately fatal disease of cats. The disease has a global distribution, and only affects cats. The first signs are often vague, and there are many possibilities, from inappetence, dullness and weight loss to abdominal swelling and difficulty breathing.

Feline Leukemia (FeLV). This deadly virus kills 85% of infected felines within three years, it can be transmitted through blood, saliva, urine and feces. This type of virus only affect cats, which means it cannot be transmitted to other animals or people. This disease can be prevented through vaccination.

Hypertrophic Cardiomyopathy (HCM). This condition causes the walls of the heart to thicken. Symptoms include tiredness and difficulty breathing. This disease can be life-threatening if undetected, however, once diagnosed it can be managed with medication that controls the heart rate and prevents clots from forming.

Obesity. The British Shorthair loves to eat but it is not overly active. Because they tend to be calm and laid-back they can be major candidates to obesity so it's always a good idea to feed them according to your breeder or vet's advice and monitor their diet.

Panleukopenia (FPV - feline distemper). This often fatal and highly contagious viral disease causes severe gastrointestinal problems including vomiting, diarrhea, bloody stool, weight loss and weakness. The virus is spread trough an infected cat's blood, feces, nasal discharge, saliva or urine. This disease can be prevented through vaccination.

Polycystic Kidney Disease (PKD). This disease causes slowly enlarging pockets of fluid (cysts) that are present at birth to form in the cat's kidneys and may not be noticed until the cat is around 7 years of age, at which time kidney functions may be compromised. However, there is no way to predict how the issue will progress in a particular cat. Persians bloodlines are usually the ones at high risk. The best way to prevent this is to rule out this gene for breeding.

Rhinotracheitis (FHV-1 - Feline Herpesvirus). This is a virus that causes upper respiratory infections (feline viral rhinotracheitis; FVR) and ocular illnesses including conjunctivitis in cats. FHV-1 infection is the most common cause of ocular problems in cats. Cats become infected through contact with saliva, ocular secretions, and nasal secretions from an infected cat. Conjunctivitis is the most common ocular condition caused by FHV-1. Cats with FHV-1 infections often have severe conjunctivitis in both eyes along with respiratory tract infections. Symptoms of conjunctivitis include squinting, swelling and redness of the eye membranes, elevated third eyelid, ocular discharge (often tan colored and pus-like). This disease can be prevented through vaccination and it cannot be transmitted to other animals or humans.

Administering Medications

Some medications come as powders that can be hidden effectively in wet food. However, If you have to give your cat a pill, I recommend you gently take hold of your cat's head from above and use the index finger of your free hand to open the cat's mouth. Put the pill as far back in the throat as you can. Gently hold the cat's mouth closed and try stroking your pet's throat to encourage swallowing. For any other kind of medications that might have to be administered in the home setting, rely on your vet's advice and ask for a demonstration. With proper instruction, any home treatment is possible.

Basic Health Care Cheklist

- ☐ *Brush your cat*. Brushing your British Shorthair regularly will help to reduce the formation of hairballs in their digestive tract. Thebest way to getting your cat to cooperate with brushing is to associate brushing with happy events. Perhaps brush them before a meal, to teach your cat to associate brushing with something tasty.
- ☐ *Watch your cat's weight*. Cats, unlike dogs, cannot be vegetarians, even for brief periods. They rely on meat as the foundation of their diets, and their main wet food meal of the day should contain some sort of meat.
- ☐ *Provide plenty of fresh water*. Domestic cats descended from desert-dwelling ancestors, so they lack the thirst-drive that dogs do. Give your cat constant access to fresh water. Cats also obtain the

majority of their water from their food, so I usually add a little bit of water to their wet food to provide them with better opportunities to stay hydrated.

☐ *Keep the litter box clean.* Keep the box as clean as possible by scooping it every day. The litter box must also be located in a suitable place. Your cat might not like it if they find their bathroom in an isolated area of the house as they want to be able to see what's happening around them and know where the quickest escaping route is.

☐ *Show where the scratching post is.* Chances are your Britsh Shorthair already know how to do this, however, if this is not the case teach your them to use a scratching post to avoid damage to valuable furniture. Place the scratch post in the center of the room. You might want to sprinkle catnip on the post when you first bring it home. After you've gotten your cat used to it, you can gradually move it to a less-trafficked location and skip the catnip.

☐ *Have your cat spayed or neutered.* There is nothing more beneficial to your cat in the long run than having them spayed or neutered. This procedure will keep them comfortable (they will not go in heat) and safe (they will not have the desire to roam outside and fight).

☐ *Travel with your pet in safety.* Even if your cat appears to prefer it, do not allow them to travel unrestrained and never leave your cat alone in a parked car.

☐ *Select a cat-friendly vet.* Seek out a veterinarian who has separate waiting areas for cats and dogs. Request to be called into the exam room as quickly as possible if your favourite veterinarian does not offer two waiting rooms.

☐ *Allow them to love you.* When a cat loves you, they will want to show you. Sometimes by bringing you the spoils of a successful hunt. Accept their gifts with grace. Your British Shortahir will also express their affection for you by head bumping, purring, or kneading you with their paws.

Human Substances That Are Poisonous To Cats

Your British Shortahir is inquisitive, poking its nose into strange places. However, their exploration may expose them to some hidden dangers in your home. It only takes a little time and know-how to cat-proof your home to keep your cat healthy and safe. Please refer to appendix A and B for a more in-depth list of harmful food and plants.

Human Medications

Some human over-the-counter and prescription medications are dangerous to cats, so keep them out of reach. These include:

- Antidepressants
- Cancer medications
- Cold medications
- Dietary supplements
- Anti-inflammatories (acetaminophen, aspirin, ibuprofen)
- Vitamins and other nutritional supplements

You may have heard that some common medications are effective for both humans and cats. However, never give your pet any pills without first consulting with your veterinarian; it's easy to give them the wrong medicine or too much, which can be fatal.

Human Food

Your cat may beg for food when you sit down to eat (or try to steal some bites when you're not looking), but some human foods are poisonous to them, including:

- Caffeine and alcohol (coffee, soda, tea)
- Chives
- Chocolate
- Garlic
- Grapes
- Onions
- Raisins
- Xylitol is a type of sugar alcohol (found in sugarless gums, candies, toothpaste)
- Dough made with yeast

Some Types of Plants

Common houseplants, as well as a few others you may bring into your home, can be harmful to your cat's health, including the following:

- Aloe
- Azalea
- Chrysanthemum
- Hyacinths
- Lily

- Marijuana
- Mistletoe
- Tulip Rhododendron Sago Palm

Chemicals and Insecticides

Some chemicals are particularly appealing to cats. Keep any chemicals locked away to keep them safe, especially:

- Antifreeze
- Bleach
- Detergents
- De-icing salts are substances that are used to prevent ice from forming on (which pets may walk through, then lick from their pads)
- Medications for fleas and ticks in dogs (pills, collars, spot-on flea treatments, sprays, shampoos)
- Fertilizers
- Herbicides
- Insect and rodent bait

Common household items that can choke or strangle your cat should be avoided. If they swallow them, they may even block their intestines.

- Bones from chicken
- Dental floss, yarn, or string are all acceptable options.
- Lights and tinsel are common holiday decorations.
- Toys that contain small or movable parts

What To Do If Your Cat Has Been Poisoned

If you suspect your cat has been exposed to something toxic, every second count. You must contact your veterinarian and gather samples as quickly as possible. Take samples of your cat's vomit, stool, and the poison he ate to the vet with you. Keep an eye out for symptoms. Cats frequently exhibit these symptoms right away. However, some symptoms may appear gradually. Among the warning signs to look out for are:

- Breathing difficulties
- Confusion
- Coughing
- Depression
- Diarrhea

- Pupils dilated
- Increased urination and drinking Increased urination Upset stomach
- a great deal of saliva
- Seizures
- Shivering
- Itching of the skin
- Tremors
- Vomiting
- Weakness

See appendix A and B for a more in-depth list of harmful food and plants.

Saving Your Cat With CPR (Cardiopulmonary Resuscitation)

No loving British Shorthair lover could ever imagine being in this situation, however, the reality is that accidents happen and knowing a little bit about how to help could save your cat's life. Classes and online videos are largely available so consider finding out more about the subject. Always remember to hold an injured cat extremely carefully as it may try to bite. If possible use a blanket of thick gloves to handle your feline friend. A first aid kit can also be very useful.

Artificial Respiration - The Heart Is Still Beating

If your cat stops breathing cardiac arrest will follow next, this is when the heart stops beating and the cat dies. However, even when breathing stops and before cardiac arrest, the heart can continue to beat for several minutes and this is when CPR can save your cat. Here is what to do if you ever find yourself in that position:

1. Place your cat on their side on a flat surface.
2. Has the cat actually stopped breathing? To be sure, a) check the rise and fall of their chest, b) feel for their breath on your hand, c) check their gums as lack of oxygen will make them turn blue.
3. Open your cat's mouth and make sure there is nothing blocking their airway. If an object is found in their throat, pull its tongue outward and use your fingers, tweezers or pliers to pull the object out. If you're unable to reach or remove the object, you will have to use the Heimlich maneuver to try and dislodge it.
4. If the cat's airway is clear, lift the cat's chin to straighten out its neck and begun rescue breathing.
5. Hold the cat's muzzle and close their mouth. Put your mouth over the

cat's nose and blow gently, just enough to cause its chest to rise.

6. Wait for the air you breathed to leave before giving another.
7. Continue the gentle breath every 3 seconds as long as the heart is still breathing and until your cat starts to breathe on their own.

CPR - The Heart Has Stopped Beating

This must be done immediately and ideally with one person performing artificial respiration while the other performs CPR.

1. Put the cat on its side.
2. Check the cat's pulse by placing your hand over its left side, just behind the front leg.
3. Place the palm of your hand on your cat's rib cage over the heart, with your other hand on top of the first. For kittens, use your thumb on one side of the chest and the rest of your fingers on the other side.
4. Press down and release, compressing the cat's chest approximately one inch (2.5 cm) and squeeze and release 80 to 100 times every minute.

CHAPTER 11

BREEDING

I have been breeding British Shorthair at Muffin & Poppy (www.muffinandpoppy.co.uk) for a decade now and can honestly say that there is only one reason to get into cat breeding: love of the breed. This is not my source of income and this is not an endeavor that will make you rich financially.

Breeding British Shorthair can be both fulfilling and challenging. It's a wonderful experience to see the little furballs develop into lovable rascals. It's extremely rewarding seeing the overwhelmingly happy faces of new kitten parents to be as they come to collect their babies. Breeding a cat should not be attempted unless you have a thorough understanding of what it takes. Many people start breeding because they think it will be fun to have a litter of kittens to play with.

Often, the importance of having healthy kittens who will need to be placed in good homes is overlooked. Caring for breeding animals properly, caring for the queen during pregnancy, queening and after delivery care of the kittens, and finding good homes for the kittens is a time-consuming and costly endeavor. Any high-quality breeder will tell you that it takes a lot of time, money, and knowledge to do it right.

Cats do not require a litter to be happy. Spaying the female before her first heat cycle eliminates the cycling, lowers her risk of mammary cancer as she ages, and eliminates the males around the house while she is in season. Even if she is used for breeding, consider spaying her after her last litter to avoid a future case of pyometra (uterus infection). Males will be more likely to spray and fight. He will be less likely to do so if he is neutered. The decrease in the smell of the urine and the frequency of spraying are two major advantages of neutering.

Do not breed unless you have healthy cats with excellent breed characteristics and are committed to the kittens for their entire lives. It's also important to note that all stud cats now require a GCCF Certificate of Entirety before any kittens can be registered. It is now a rule that one must be obtained before any visiting queen is accepted. There is a financial penalty if you do not[1].

What Age Should A Cat Be Before Breeding?

Before a male can breed, he should be at least 18 months old. This gives us time to see if he's healthy and ready to breed. Temperament, as well as genetic diseases, are passed down to offspring. Make an appointment for a physical exam, vaccinations, a stool check for internal parasites, and any other necessary tests before the breeding season begins. Before each breeding, both parents should be tested for FeLV and FIV. They should be in good health and free of parasites such as ear mites, fleas, and ringworm. Genetic conditions such as polycystic kidney disease, hip dysplasia, patellar locations, and heart disease should be tested for cats. These tests should be performed before breeding. Check with your veterinarian to see if any other breed-specific diseases should be tested before breeding.

Female cats should be at least 18-24 months old and at her ideal weight. Those who are overweight or underweight may have more difficulty conceiving, carrying the litter, and queening. In addition to physical health, the parents' personalities can also be important because they can play a significant role in determining the kittens' personalities. If the parents are laid-back and friendly, the kittens are likely to be as well. If the parents are aggressive or fearful of people and other animals, the kittens are likely to be as well.

Breeding Risks

Disease. If not well looked after the queen and the kittens could develop diseases. Young kittens should remain in a warm, clean and safe environment and the queen should not be allowed out of the nursery to prevent diseases. I usually keep the mother cat with their kittens for at least 2-3 weeks. I only let them out for short cuddles and little walks in a very limited safe and sterilised area to prevent diseases. DO NOT allow your queen to roam outside even if you have an enclosed garden as birds can spread diseases too. As a breeder you want to prevent disease at all cost. Diseases can be carried by air, shoes, other household or wild animals and clothes to name a few. I cannot emphasise this enough - Be highly aware of diseases and parasites.

Kitten Death. This rarely happens, but there is a chance that not all kittens will make it before three days after birth. After three days they are safe. Kittens must be kept in a clean, warm environment at all times until they leave to their permanent homes.

Market Demand. Can you find forever homes for your kittens?

The Heat Cycle Of A Cat

A female cat usually has her first season at 5 - 8 months of age. This is proestrus, often referred to as calling. When she is ready to mate she will become very vocal, rolling, treading her hind legs and sometimes looking and sounding as if she is in pain. There will be no noticeable vaginal discharge or swelling. This could last 1 - 2 days. The first observed mating may not necessarily be the first successful mating. If she mates successfully she ovulates automatically and in most cases becomes pregnant. If she doesn't mate she will come into proestrus again every 21 days throughout the breeding season (normally January-May and July-September). Pregnancy lasts for 9 weeks.

Queens are seasonally polyestrous, which means they come into heat at different times of the year. If they are not bred, they will cycle multiple times. They are also reflex ovulators, which means they must be bred before ovulating. Cycling is most common in outdoor cats during the spring and summer. Cats that are kept indoors and exposed to artificial lights can cycle all year. proestrus, estrus, diestrus, and anestrus (or interestrus) are the stages of a cat's estrus cycle. Anestrus is most common during the winter's short days. The sire has no feelings for the queen and vice versa[2]. Proestrus may last 1-2 days in some queens, but it cannot always be observed. She may call the sire, roll, and rub on the ground during this stage. She will not let the sire pass her by. Female cats do not experience the proestrus bleeding that female dogs do. She could go from proestrus to estrus in a matter of hours. Estrus usually lasts about 3 to 16 days, but it can last longer or shorter. The queen should be introduced to the sire for mating. The queen will allow the sire to approach her and mate during this time. Mating can last anywhere from 1 to 20 seconds. After breeding the queen, the sire must have an escape route, such as a box or shelf to jump on, because she often responds aggressively. She will frantically groom herself immediately after mating and refuse to let the sire near her for up to an hour. Her receptive behavior and mating will resume after that. In one study, three breedings per day for the first three days of estrus resulted in ovulation in 90 percent of the queens. During estrus, the queen may allow more than one sire to mate with her; a litter of kittens may have multiple fathers (superfecundation)[3]. She would enter an interfollicular stage if she was not bred (also known as interests). During this stage, she shows no signs of reproductive activity. This stage could last up to a week. She then enters proestrus and then estrus. If the mating was successful, she would be pregnant for about 63 days but pregnancy can be as short as 57 days or as long as 70 days[4]. Calculate her due date by adding 63 days to the last day of mating. If her estrus cycle lasted a week and bred every other day, her due date would also be spread out over a week. If a female has an abortion or loses her nursing kittens, she will go into estrus again in 2-3 weeks. She will resume cycling after having a litter when the kittens are 8 to 10 weeks old. To the untrained eye, cat mating appears simple: they mate loudly, frequently, and indiscriminately; the female cat becomes pregnant, then gives birth to anything from one to six kittens, although a litter of nine or even twelve is also possible. Mating is an interesting subject when it comes to cats. Did you know, for example, that cats do not ovulate until they mate? Or that a female cat can have kittens from different fathers and male cats have barbed penises to stimulate female cats to ovulate?

Pregnancy And Conception

Female cats that have not been spayed will eventually go into heat (proestrus). A kitten can have its first heat as early as at 3 months of age and once a female cat has her first heat, it will repeatedly occur until she either mates or is spayed. It's important to ensure that your cat is well nourished during pregnancy and especially after, during her period of milk production. Also, test your cat and the proposed father to ensure that they are not carriers of viral diseases such as FIV and FeLV. The size of a litter can influence the length of gestation. Larger litters are often associated with a shorter gestation time (Burmese & Asians) whereas smaller litters or single kittens may be associated with a longer gestation (Somali). This may be partly due to weaker uterine stimulation. Other factors known to influence litter size are the reproductive age and stage of development, hereditary factors, the presence of disease, bacterial infection, trauma and the nutritional status of the queen. Stress can also play its part[5].

Symptoms That Your Cat Is Pregnant

Cats in heat will go to any length to find a male cat with whom to mate. If your cat was in heat and had access to an un-neutered male cat, the chances are she is pregnant. A pregnant queen will undergo physical and psychological changes that will become apparent three weeks after mating. Recognize the signs that your cat is pregnant.

- Heat cycles cease
- Nipples swell and become rosier in color
- Appetite increases
- Weight gain
- Nesting
- Vomiting
- Enlarged abdomen

- Affection increases
- Increase in sleeping

Taking Care Of Your Cat While Pregnant

The greatest risk to unborn kittens occurs during the first three weeks of development in the womb. Both drugs and infections can impair healthy development. Exposure to feline infectious enteritis (FIE) and panleukopenia, for example, can cause the kittens to be with severe brain damage. Your queen should also be vaccinated before she gets pregnant to increase the chance of passive protection they will pass in the first milk. Never give medications or vaccinate pregnant cats or other household cats as the live vaccine virus can be shed by vaccinated cats and affect the pregnant cat's foetuses[6]. You'll want to make sure your pregnant British Shorthair is in a safe and exclusive enclosure and has everything she needs, both for her own health and the health of her unborn kittens. Except for nutritional considerations, which are especially important for a pregnant cat, the majority of the things you'll provide for her are the same as you would for any cat in your care: shelter, a place to sleep, a litter box, a scratching post, and toys (Exercise is also important for pregnant cats).

Signs Your Cat Will Give Birth Soon

Once active labor starts, try to leave her undisturbed. Watch from a safe distance to make sure she does not go into distress. These signs indicates kittens are on the way:

- Nesting Activities
- Restlessness
- Vocalization
- Lowered Body Temperature
- Loss of Appetite
- Vulva Licking

Potential Issues In Cat Pregnancy

Although pregnant cats usually have trouble-free pregnancies, some issues can arise. In general, any unusual symptoms during pregnancy should be followed up with a phone call or visit to your veterinarian.

Assisting Your Cat During the Birth Process

Most likely, you will not need to do anything to assist with the birth process other than being present with your cat to encourage her. About 30 to 60 minutes may pass between births, but more prolonged periods are not uncommon. You might even wake up in the morning to find that your pregnant cat has given birth during the night and is happily nursing her kittens.

Birthing Dos and Don'ts

Do
- Ensure that the queen (the mother cat) is comfortable and has enough space in a warm nest. A clean and spacious cardboard with a warm towel should work fine.
- This is rare but if a kitten is partly out, and the mother is very tired and the kitten isn't passed within a few seconds, you can gently try to pull them out by pulling downwards very gently with clean hands.
- Count the placentas each kitten should have one.
- Gently and without stress, ensure that kittens are feeding after delivery is over.
- Have your vet's number ready.

Don't
- Disturb the queen. Keep her calm and use a gentle voice if you want to support her.
- Pull the kitten's placenta out as this could kill the queen.
- Allow other animals or unsupervised children in the area.

Mother Cat And Newborns Postnatal Care

The first two to three weeks are critical. The kittens should be growing quickly. Keep the mother and her babies in a quiet part of the house, preferably a separate room, and make sure the room is warm enough. One of the most serious dangers to newborn kittens is chilling. Allow the mother cat to dictate the pace of your attention. If she has been her companion and resident for a long time, she may welcome your visits. Also, it's important not to distract her or let her out of her pen as she must focus on the new kittens.

The Kitten Season

Easily one of the cutest and most joyful seasons you will ever experience! During kitten season you will need to:

- Prevent outside animals to be in contact with the queen or kittens. This also applies to people that have been in touch with outside animals.
- Have a safe and warm place to keep the kittens.
- Lower food/water bowls and kitten litter tray.
- Welcome potential buyers to see the kitten in a presentable environment.
- Welcome kitten visits for people that have already paid their deposit.
- Take the kittens to the vet at 9 and 12 weeks.
- Keep the kittens' paperwork safe and tidy.

Weekly Kitten Development

Week 1 - Stay with mom and practice grooming.
Week 2 - Eyes open and playing starts. Kittens practice walking.
Week 3 - Litter training starts. Kittens play, walk and groom themselves more fluently. It's possible to sex kittens at this stage.
Week 4 - Introduce water. Kittens try to jump out the box. They are suitable for viewing (but not touching) around this stage.
Week 5 - Weaning and advanced litter training starts. Get kittens used to pet carriers by allowing them in.
Week 6 - Kittens play hard and start eating solid food.
Week 7 - Kittens can purr!!!
Week 8 - Getting cutter and cutter every day!
Week 9 - 1st Vaccine and Microchipping.
Week 10 - Kittens routine = Play, eat, sleep.
Week 11 - Munchkins getting ready for their new home. Get your heart ready.
Week 12 - 2nd Vaccine, Defleeing/Deworming.
Week 13 - Permanent home.

Kittens Usual Daily Routine

09:30 - 10:30 Feed and nap
10:30 - 11:30 Playtime!
11:30 - 12:30 Feed and nap
12:30 - 13:00 Socialise
13:00 - 13:30 Feed and nap
13:00 - 14:00 Feed
14:00 - 15:00 More playtime!
16:00 - 17:30 Feed and nap

Finding A Suitable Forever Home

Depending on how you handle the preparations, sending kittens away to a new forever home can be either a joyful or a worrying experience. You've put in three months or more of work, worry, and probably money to care for the mother cat and the kittens. Their futures will be determined by your willingness to invest a little more time ensuring that the new homes they will be moving into are truly good. Here are some question to ask potential parents:

- Who will be the main person responsible for the kitten?
- Do you have children? If so, do they know how to interact with the new addition?
- Do you have other pets? If so, are they used to other animals and do you have an introduction plan ready?
- Do you understand the basics of caring for a new pet? Do you know what to NOT feed them?

CHAPTER 12

THE IMPORTANCE OF PET INSURANCE

Pet insurance is a policy purchased by a pet owner that helps to reduce the overall costs of expensive vet bills. This coverage is comparable to human health insurance policies. Pet insurance will cover the often-expensive veterinary procedures, either entirely or partially. It is necessary to evaluate and compare pet insurance plans to find the best plan for you[1]. The majority of providers will base the insurance premium on the average cost of veterinary care in the owner's region. Furthermore, the policy might not cover all veterinary procedures. Also, pet insurance functions more like property insurance than health insurance. Reimbursement works a little differently than the regularly accepted human model:

- You pay the vet.
- You fill in the claim.
- You receive the reimbursement directly.

The reimbursement will include eligible expenses minus the level of your deductible and copy according to the limits of your policy. A comprehensive insurance policy for a British Shorthair kitten, including coverage for accidents, illnesses, and some hereditary conditions with an option for chronic condition coverage, can be purchased for about £12 - £20 ($15 - $26) per month, depending on the deductible chosen.

Pet Insurance Price

A pet owner can purchase a policy that will save some out-of-pocket expenses to help with yearly costs and unexpected emergencies. A pet owner will pay a yearly or monthly premium, similar to how people pay for health insurance. Some of the factors that influence the cost of pet insurance are as follows:

- *Species.* Dogs usually cost more than cats because they are larger and receive more claims.
- *Breed.* Some breeds are more prone to certain illnesses and injuries than others.
- *Gender.* Because males file more claims than females, females are less expensive.
- *Age.* The older the pet, the more expensive the insurance.
- *Location.* Insurance is dearer in metropolitan areas than in the suburbs and rural areas.

Most companies have three insurance tiers. There is accident-only, or basic coverage, which typically costs about £9 ($12) per month; accident and illness, or comprehensive coverage, which typically costs about £21 ($29) per month; and wellness coverage, which typically costs about £18 ($25) per month. Insurance will not cover the entire cost of medical treatment. The average co-pay is 80% of the claim amount. Still, some companies advertise that they offer 90% or even 100% coverage on certain procedures[2]. The cost of insurance may outweigh the cost of services for young cats who only require yearly checkups. However, if an emergency occurs, the cost of veterinary care may exceed the insurance premium. It's also important to note that because senior pets require more procedures, the coverage could save money whether there is an emergency or not.

The Origins of Pet Insurance

Pet insurance first appeared in Sweden in 1924, reaching Britain in 1947. In 1980 a company called Veterinary Pet Insurance (VPI) opened its doors as the first and only company at the time that offered pet insurance policies in North America[3]. In 1982 the canine movie star Lassie was the first dog in the United States to receive a pet insurance policy . The product's popularity has then grown since its inception[4].

The Benefits of Pet Insurance

Compared to health insurance policies written for humans, comprehending your pet policy is a much simpler task. Consider the following benefits:
- *Choice of vet.* Pet insurers will not tell you who you can and cannot see

as long as the vet is licensed. There are no out-of-network doctors, as your health insurance policy most likely requires.

- *Simple procedures.* Most businesses only have three tiers from which to choose.
- *Low-cost premiums.* The cost of insurance varies depending on the coverage and policy. The cost is determined by various factors, including the breed and age of the animal, where you live, and the options you select as part of your policy.

Is Pet Insurance Worth It?

Typically such policy carries about £9,000 ($12,000) a year in benefits and is renewable annually. Ask plenty of questions to determine the best company and plan for your needs:

- Can you go to your regular vet, or do you have to go to a vet assigned by the pet insurance company?
- What does the insurance plan cover? Does it cover annual exams? Surgeries? Emergency illness and injury?
- Does coverage begin immediately?
- Are pre-existing conditions covered? In addition, if your cat develops a health issue and you later have to renew the policy, is that condition covered when you renew your policy?
- Is medication covered?
- Do you have to have pre-authorization before your pet receives treatment? What happens if your cat has the treatment without pre-authorization?
- Does the insurance policy cover dental issues and chronic health problems?
- Is there a lifetime maximum benefit amount? If so, how much is that amount? A benefit plan with a lifetime maximum of only a few hundred dollars surely will not suffice!
- Is there an amount that you have to pay before the insurance pays out?

If you don't want to use the same company recommended by the breeder take the time to research your pet insurance options. Compare the different plans available, what each covers, and the cost before deciding which is best for you and your pet. While pet insurance may not be a feasible option for you, consider having a backup plan, just in case your cat requires emergency care, or you run into unexpected veterinarian costs. A simple way to prepare for an emergency is to start a veterinary fund for your British Shorthair.

Decide to put a certain amount of money aside each month. Think about the potential financial costs of veterinary care and plan for how you will pay for it now. Do not wait until something happens.

Planning For An Emergency

It brings great comfort and peace of mind knowing that our beloved fluffy companions will be properly cared for if something happens to us. Some mobile/cell phones allow you to input an ICE (In Case of Emergency) number with notes. If this is not an option, write the information below on a piece of paper and put it in your wallet with your driver's license:

- The names of each of your cats.
- The names and phone numbers of family members or friends who have agreed to temporarily care for your cats in an emergency.
- The name and phone number of your veterinarian.

It can also be helpful to talk with your neighbors and family, letting them know how many cats you have. That way, if something happens to you, they can alert the authorities, ensuring your cats do not stay by themselves for days before they are found. Instructions for the intended guardians can also be useful. Also, be sure to provide each individual with a key to your home (talk to your home insurance company first so that this does not affect your coverage).

Instructions should include:

- The name and phone numbers of each individual who agreed to take care of your cat.
- Your cat's diet and feeding schedule.
- The name and phone number of your vet.
- Any health problems and medications your cat may take, including dosage instructions, instructions on how to give the medicine, and where it is kept.

Put as much relevant information as necessary to ensure the guardians can provide the same level of care that you did.

PART 4: LIVING WITH YOUR COMPANION

CHAPTER 13

TRAVELLING WITH YOUR BRITISH SHORTHAIR

Some cats travel better than others. While one whimsical blue may panic and lash out at the sight of a pet carrier, another may simply enjoy travel and the open road. Although there is a lot of variation between individuals, the calm, collected British Shorthair is generally one of the easiest breeds to travel with. Whether you're planning a quick weekend break with your British Shorthair, a fortnight-long road trip, or even a week-long holiday or transatlantic travel preparation is the key to a successful journey. You can avoid a lot of problems by doing your homework and planning ahead of time. Here are three things you must do:

1. *Consult your vet.* It is advisable to consult your veterinarian before embarking on any trip, especially if you will be travelling internationally. Your veterinarian can assist you by administering any necessary vaccinations for your cat and addressing any health issues that may jeopardize your pet's ability to travel. Your veterinarian may be able to provide you with useful advice on travelling with your cat. Also, while travelling, make sure you know where you can get emergency veterinary care. Find out if a veterinarian is near your destination and note any veterinarian offices along the way.
2. *Get your cat used to the mode of transportation you'll be using.* Start with short drives and work your way up to longer ones if you're travelling by car. The same process applies to travelling by bus or train. This will help your cat relax on their epic voyage because the noises, scents, and sights will be familiar and so less likely to cause stress.
3. *Reward your cat with a small snack or favourite food.* Once your cat acclimated to the short trip show them how good they are. You can even schedule the trip around her regular mealtime so they associate

the experience of travelling with a tasty bowl of yummy food. British Shorthairs love their food, so if you can make them associate travel with a nice meal, They'll be much more willing to oblige. Ideally, you should begin the process as far ahead of time as possible — at least a few weeks. These trial runs can help you detect any travel concerns your pompous British Shorthair may have.

Motion Sickness

Motion sickness is a common problem that can be difficult to detect on short trips. Even if your British Shorthair does not vomit, they may be in a lot of pain if they become seasick. Your cat may be suffering from motion sickness if they start crying and don't stop after a few minutes. Motion sickness in cats can also manifest as excessive drooling, rigid immobility, or signs of fear and anxiety. If your little companion gets very sick, they may also lose control of their bowels or bladder. Motion sickness does not usually lead to serious medical problems in cats. However, vomiting or diarrhea can lead to dehydration. Ask your vet about motion sickness cures when you take your cat in for a pre-trip checkup. Try out the treatment before the main trip to ensure it doesn't work or generate an unfavourable reaction. In certain situations, a different method of transportation may be more agreeable to your cat; for example, cats who feel sick on buses or in vehicles typically do well on trains. Some veterinarians may offer a sedative in addition to motion sickness remedies to help keep your cat relaxed during a long journey. This could be as easy as an over-the-counter antihistamine, but for really anxious cats, a veterinarian may prescribe something stronger. Sedatives should only be used as a last resort if non-medical alternatives fail. You should think about your alternatives carefully and always test the sedative at home. You'll be able to observe how it affects your cat and make sure they don't react negatively. On a long train or airline travel, a bad sedative reaction would be considerably more difficult to deal with than at home.

Motion Sickness Diagnosis

During a car ride, cats suffering from motion sickness may exhibit gastrointestinal issues such as drooling, vomiting and diarrhea. Your British Shorthair can also show signs of stress and anxiety, including agitation, panting, lethargy and excessive vocalization. Your cat may also resist entering the carrier or vehicle due to motion sickness.

Getting Your Cat Ready For The Pet Carrier

It is critical to prepare your cat's carrier or pen and ensure that your companion is happy to enter it. Don't introduce the carrier too quickly. You must give your cat time to get used to it. You can lay a soft towel or a small pet blanket on your cat's bed or favorite sleeping spot to pick up the cat's familiar scent and pheromones. The blanket, when placed in your cat's carrier, will make it feel like home. You may also consider putting the entire bed inside if the carrier is large enough. Placing their food dish inside is another way to encourage your cat to enter the pet carrier. I usually train my cats to get used to their carriers by leaving them open in their area around the house as a first step, so they can go in and out freely without much fuss. These suggestions, if followed, should familiarize your cat with the feel and smell of the carrier while also associating it with food in their mind. The famous British Shorthair appetite will come to your aid once more. If your cat likes catnip, put a pinch or two in the carrier and make sure your cat has a favorite toy in her carrier on the day of travel.

When choosing a cat carrier, take your time. For a one-time trip, such as a change of address or vet visits, your regular carrier will most likely suffice, as long as you won't be on the road for more than a few hours. Check that the carrier you choose meets the requirements for the train or airline you're taking. So, always aim for sturdy, comfortable carriers that meet the majority of airline requirements.

Harness training your British Shorthair cat will be highly beneficial if you want to travel with them on a frequent basis. Cats are generally resistant to wearing a harness and being led. Even so, the British Shorthair can be trained to tolerate, even enjoy, being walked in a harness. A harness-trained cat can be easily removed from the carrier and allowed to stretch its legs without fear of them running away and becoming lost. Some cats are terrified of new environments, but others are incredibly curious and will thoroughly enjoy a quick stroll around a rest stop. A good harness also provide you with something to grab onto if your cat manages to get out of her carrier when she isn't supposed to. In the next chapter you will find out more about how to harness train your cat.

Consider what you're going to do about the litter-box situation ahead of time. If your cat is traveling in a large enough pen and you don't anticipate a rough ride, you might consider putting a small litter box inside the pen. If not, make sure the pen or carrier is well-lined with newspaper or puppy pads and that all of the contents can be easily washed. The litter box can be kept outside the carrier if access to it is quickly provided after the trip is over.

Car Travel Checklist

- ☐ Give your cat car time every day a few weeks before your trip. You may want to do this in a closed garage or enclosed garden to prevent your British Shorthair from fleeing. Alternatively, a harness could help keep your cat safe. Allow your precious fluffball to safely sniff around inside the car. Keep you car with the door open to facilitate an easy exit. Place their bedding on the seat, take them into the car, close the door, and spend some time with them in the car. Take them out to the car after feeding them and place their food bowl on the floor of the car.

☐ Sprinkle a pinch of catnip on the floor or seat where you intend to strap the carrier. Do this only if your cat enjoys catnip. I prefer to use catnip in a spray for best results. Be careful with other pheromones as they may cause a negative reaction such as scratching or spraying.

☐ Take your cat on short trial journeys once they are comfortable in the car.

☐ Repeat the above process if your British Shorthair gets upset when you drive them around. Allow them more time to adjust and keep a supply of really good treats and food that they enjoy.

Main Trip Tips

- Feed your cat three to four hours before the trip. This will give them time to use the litter box while also preventing them from becoming nauseous or hungry on the road.
- Take your cat for a walk (if she's harness trained). Alternatively, engage them in some vigorous play to help burn off energy and get them ready for a nap before the trip.
- Make sure the carrier is well-stocked with comfortable bedding, a toy or two, and perhaps a treat for the road.
- Administer any anti-nausea or sedative medications as prescribed by your vet, allowing enough time for them to take effect before the trip begins. When taking your cat outside, cover their pen or carrier with a blanket. Nervous cats can become anxious when they see and smell unfamiliar environments.

Transport And Accommodation

Even if your cat is safely settled in their carrier, don't assume that your airline, train, or bus company will automatically allow them on board. Rules and policies differ from one company to the next. Some companies have strict pet policies that will require your British Shorthair to travel in a baggage compartment.

WARNING: Do NOT try to sneak your cat onto a bus, train, or another mode of transportation without permission! This could have a very messy and even fatal ending.

☐ Do you fully understand the travel company's current policies and regulations? Do this well before you book your tickets. Make sure you clearly understand policies and regulations and double-check everything before leaving. If possible have everything in writing. This is crucial if you're taking your British Shorthair on a trip abroad; you'll need to verify the rules for transporting animals into your destination country, as well as the requirements for your airline, train, local bus, and other modes of transportation.

☐ Does your hotel or lodging allow pets? If the hotel allows pets, find out their rules and any extra fees for bringing your cat. While some hotels allow your cat to stay in your suite, others require her to stay in on-site pet accommodations. Look for reviews and recommendations from other cat owners who have stayed there before you.

☐ Do you have a good supply of food and water? Bear in mind that dry food can be easier and less messy to transport than wet food pouches. Is the food you feed your cat available in your destination?

☐ Do you have food and water bowls? Disposable plastic or paper is fine as long as you do not reuse them as germs can live in them.

☐ Have you packed your pet's favourite toys, bed or blanket?

☐ Have you included a small litter tray, litter, a scooper, odour-elimination bags, and preferably a container with a lid to keep them in until you can find a way to dispose of them?

☐ Do you have your cat's identification tags, medication, and vaccination records? These items may be required on some journeys, such as traveling between states in the United States or boarding a plane.

☐ Has your cat been microchipped? Is your pet wearing an identifying collar?

Travelling By Bus Or Train

Many long-distance bus or coach lines prohibit all animals except trained service animals. Please note that untrained emotional support animals are usually prohibited too. You will not be allowed to board the bus with your British Shorthair, no matter how much you beg or how adorable they are. Saying that, smaller local bus lines may allow you to bring your cat as long as they're properly secured in the pet carrier; there may even be a small charge, so check with the bus company first. You should be able to place your cat in the carrier on your lap or on the seat next to you, but don't be surprised if you are asked to keep it on the floor and not on the seat. Alternatively, place your Brit in a designated baggage area at eye level and sit nearby. It's possible that you'll be able to transport your cat by train. Normally, there are certain limitations for the carrier you can use and again there may be a fee involved. This varies widely between companies; some place weight restrictions on pets or refuse to transport them on longer trips. Many train operators require vaccination records for animals travelling on their trains, so make sure you carry current documentation with you. If possible, avoid travelling at peak times and always check in advance to find out if you will need a separate ticket for your companion.

Travelling By Plane

Is it safe to fly with my British Shorthair? Yes, as long as you are well-prepared.

Air Travel Checklist

- ☐ Do you know how your cat will be travelling? You must confirm if your cat can travel in the aircraft cabin under the seat in front of you. You will need the precise weight requirements and dimensions under the airline seat as this will dictate the size of your pet carrier. Always make sure your cat is secure in an airline-approved airplane pet carrier and does not bolt. Keep the door closed until you are in an enclosed space. Ask the airline for a locator number for your cat that is associated with your seat number. Avoid putting your cat in the cargo hold unless you have several cats or a particularly vocal and aggressive one, although this should not be a problem with British Shorthairs. It's also a good idea to take your British Shorthair on a few shorter flights beforehand so that both of you can get used to the new situation. I would not recommend leaving snacks in the pet carrier as cats should not eat on airplanes.
- ☐ Do you know the airline policy? Speak to the airline about travelling with cats to find out what their particular policies are on taking a cat on a plane. Ask specifically about where your cat will be for the journey (they'll most likely be in the cargo area), what type of regulations your cat basket needs to meet, how often food will be dispensed and whether they have any rules about the age or medical condition of your cat. Do not travel with any cat under 3 months of age, an elderly cat, a pregnant cat or a cat that's in poor health.
- ☐ If you're planning to travel abroad with more than one cat, it's a good

idea to give them their own separate cat transporters. Even best friends can get on each other's nerves on a long flight!

☐ Do you know how much the ticket will cost? You will need to purchase a ticket for your cat.

☐ Do you know what paperwork you must have in preparation for travel? This includes vaccination records and a health certificate for travel.

Things To Consider

Try to get your cat onto as direct a flight as possible to avoid them having to be moved between planes and consider the airline's schedule to avoid arriving at a time of day when it's either really hot or extremely cold.

Some flights aren't licensed to carry animals so double-check that you'll be flying on the same plane as your cat.

Allow your cat to use her litter box before you leave for the airport.

DO NOT allow your cat to pass through the X-ray machine — it is not permitted and is highly dangerous. Send the carrier first then go through the screening with your cat. If security personnel insist, the carrier may pass; the cat must be carefully carried through the metal detector. Hang onto the cat's lead as it may take the opportunity to bolt.

Consider a soft-sided travel carrier as it is more flexible when fitting under the airline seat space. You can get your cat used to the carrier by feeding your cat in the carrier. Have the carrier open and available in your home and make it as inviting as possible. Practice entry and exit from the carrier to make it as routine a process as possible – this will be important during security screening. Ideally, the airline-approved carrier for your British Shorthair should fit under the seat in front of you or on the seat next to you. Try not to interact with your cat too much as they will need to remain calm and quiet in their carrier until the journey is over.

When traveling with your cat, ensure that your pet wears a collar with two identification tags. One tag should list your name, telephone number, and address. The other tag should list the name, telephone number, and address of a secondary contact person. For extra security, you can also attach a travel label to the outside of your cat's carrier containing your name, address, phone number, destination, and the information where you or another contact person can be reached when the flight lands and attach Live Animal stickers to the outside of your cat's carrier as well[1].

You can also withhold breakfast on the day of travel to minimise the risk of nausea and vomiting. Line the carrier with an absorbent kitten pad in case your cat needs to urinate or defecate during travel. Carry extra pads as well as a couple of zip-lock bags, some paper towels, and a few pairs of latex gloves for any necessary cleanup and containment of a mess. Carry some of your cat's food with you, a water bottle and bowl, and do not forget to bring any medications they need.

Cats usually travel quite well without the need for medication. Consult your vet, however, if yours doesn't like travelling. Strategies to de-stress feline flights include:

- A Thundershirt® which swaddles the cats much like swaddling a baby to reduce anxiety[2].
- Feliway® pheromone wipes and spray can be used in the carrier prior to flying can help lower anxiety.
- A pheromone calming collar can help to lower anxiety.
- Buprenorphine (brand names Buprenex®, Simbadol®), gabapentin (brand name Neurontin®), and alprazolam (brand names: Xanax®, Niravam®) are examples of medications that are sometimes prescribed by vets to reduce the anxiety that some cats experience when travelling. Be sure to provide a dose at home ahead of time to know how your cat will react to the medication.

Travelling By Car

You have more control over variables when transporting your British Shorthair by car. It's also much easier to transport all of your cat's equipment if you can fit it in the boot. You should not have any trouble training your cat to ride in the car with you, with time they will even enjoy it. Your cat should travel in the car with you (not in the boot) in a suitable carrier that is securely fastened to the car seat. In the event of a sudden stop or an accident, the carrier should not shift or be thrown out of the seat.

Travelling By Motorhome (RV)

The rules stated above also apply to motorhomes and caravans - Your cat must be properly secured in the carrier when the vehicle is in motion. The difference is that your cat will need to be out of the carrier when you are not driving. Get your cat used to the motorhome in the same way you would a car. Let them explore inside at their leisure, place their bedding on the seats, and feed them in the motorhome. Take your cat on longer and longer drives to get them used to being strapped into the seat in the pet carrier.

Make sure your cat is in their pet carrier or on a secure lead when you open your motorhome door. Perhaps invest in a larger pet pen with more room for your cat to move around. This should be big enough for your British Shorthair to stand up, turn around, and stretch out. The litter box and bed can also be placed in the pen.

Staying At A Hotel

When you arrive at the hotel don't leave your cat alone. They will need time to adjust to the room from the safety of the pet carrier. Talk to your cat and allow them to see you; give them a treat or two to comfort them. Spray the room or plug in the diffuser if your cat responds well to pheromone therapy. Introduce your British Shorthair to the room once they appear settled and relaxed. I would recommend to put your cat in a harness for this; even the most steadfast British Shorthair can overreact to being in an unfamiliar environment and run off to hide somewhere. Being a cat, they will teleport themselves to the most inaccessible location in the room. Don't spend the first night trying to get them out of their fort but allow them to walk around on the lead and sniff everything so they feel at ease. If you need to leave the room for any reason, make sure they have used the litter and give them lots of attention first and cover the carrier to make them feel more at ease, your companion should then be fine for an hour or two. British Shorthairs are incredibly self-sufficient cats who flourish when left alone. If your cat will be alone, it's a good idea to make sure she has a lot of familiar stuff with her. I would not recommend leaving your cat in the carrier if you're going out for the day. It's also a good idea to remove the Do Not Disturb sign from your door and post a message on it informing housekeeping employees that there is a cat in the room reminding them not to open the pet carrier.

Alternatively, leave your companion in the bathroom with the litter box, food, bed, and other belongings. The bathroom is a calm location with an easy-to-clean floor and little or no upholstery to claw if she becomes unsettled. Place a note on the bathroom door advising housekeeping that there is a cat loose in the bathroom and that they should not open the door if she escapes. Some pet-friendly hotels may even provide cat-sitting if you're lucky. Always, give your cat full attention and play with them before you leave.

Time Away From Your Cat

If it were up to us all of our British Shorthairs would permanently be with us wherever we went. However, the harsh reality is that sometimes that is not always possible. We must consider what we will do with our fuzzball before such a time arrives. Here are some questions to ask:

Who would be willing to look after my cat for me? Do I have a responsible friend or family member that would be willing to catsit? Is my cat familiar with this person?

Do I have the contact for a reliable petsitter? Has this person been recommended? Can I find past clients' experiences about this person? Do they have experience with cats? Am I comfortable with this person? Is this person insured? Do I need to inform my home insurance provider? Some useful sites include: petsitters.org (USA), dogsit.com (UK), petsit.com (Int.).

Will the person looking after my cat have access to clean water and enough food? I recommend you leave enough food stored for at least another week or two to prevent inconvenience for the person looking after your cat and peace of mind for when you get back home, knowing that you don't need to stop for cat food on the way home.

Should I contact a cattery or boarding organisation instead? Does my breeder or vet offer boarding? Please note that catteries are usually booked quickly, so it's a good idea to plan your trip carefully and way ahead of time when considering boarding your cat. Cats usually like quiet places so a good question to ask is: Is this a cattery? Catteries are more suited to look after your cats than general places. Some will even have bird watching as a feature for your cat and warm beds. Look for the best and don't be afraid to ask questions. What are the sleeping and food arrangements? Is there a vet on staff? Do you require vaccinations boosters and medical records prior to stay? Reputable catteries will require them. Can I see the enclosures? If I bring more than one can they stay together? Can I have a copy of your policy? Are you registered? Where do I find more information? The key is to know clearly what's expected of you and what you can expect from them. If possible in writing.

Travelling To The EU

I highly recommend you check the latest government advice about travelling from Great Britain to Northern Ireland or the European Union with your cat.

EU Travel Checklist

- ☐ Ensure your cat is microchipped.
- ☐ Ensure that your cat is vaccinated against rabies – pets must be at least 12 weeks old before they can be vaccinated.
- ☐ Wait 21 days after the primary vaccination before travel.
- ☐ Visit your vet to get an animal health certificate (AHC) for your cat, no more than 10 days before travelling to the EU.

IMPORTANT: Always check the latest government advice[3] and the airlines and airports you can use before travelling[4]. Also, make sure you visit the Department for Environment, Food and Rural Affairs (DEFRA) website to find out the entry requirements for the country you're planning to go to[5]. The IATA website (www.iata.org) also provides useful information for cat owners[6].

CHAPTER 14

Training Ground Rules For Your Cat

When you bring home your new kitten, they will be relying on your guidance to teach them what they might not have already learned from their mother. I must also remind you that you are not buying a plug and play device. Little accidents can happen. I must emphasize that kittens are not battery operated toys, they are little creatures that will have to adapt to major changes when they leave to their new homes. Your British Shorthair is quite smart and able to learn from a young age. The main thing is to be patient and contact the breeder in case you need any tips. This book and our muffinandpoppy.co.uk website should also provide you with excellent information on how to be a great cat parent.

Free Feeding And Scheduled Feeding

Free feeding means leaving dry food in the bowl for your cat, allowing him to eat as much as your cat chooses. The advantage is that when you're out the whole day, you don't have to rush home to feed your starving cat. The disadvantage is that your cat can become overweight, especially if you use a food dispenser.

Scheduled feeding means controlled portions at fixed times. This is doable if you have a predictable schedule or work from home. Feeding your cat doesn't have to be difficult. Cats have a strong sense of routine. We can take advantage of this fact by developing and adhering to a regular feeding schedule. Regularly feeding an adult cat provides the security and predictability of a routine. Meals become the focal point of the day, around which other activities revolve. A feeding schedule assists your cat in adjusting to changes in the household (e.g. a child moves away to college, a new baby arrives, or a holiday during which a house-sitter is in charge). A feeding routine also facilitates a necessary food change. When your cat is used to eating at the same times every day, their body learns to anticipate food at those times. Hunger can be an excellent motivator. Suppose the stage is set for increased hunger followed by regular meals. In that case, transitioning to a new food is often simple and painless.

Cats, like humans, have simple stomach anatomy. Because cats have a simple stomach structure, food will move into the small intestine, and the stomach will empty within a few hours. An empty stomach sends messages to the brain after 8 to 10 hours, producing a hunger response. As a result, your cat should eat at least two meals every day.

Positive Reinforcement

Positive reinforcement is a popular term in psychology and involves the use of positive stimuli to modify behavior. This method can be used when training and teaching your cat to abandon an unhealthy habit. Positive reinforcement focuses on reinforcing stimuli following a behavior that makes it more likely that the behavior will repeat again in the future. At that time, a favorable action or behavior and desired response strengthen thanks to the addition of a reward. In cat training, rewards are snacks, verbal praise but also a positive approach toward behavior changes.

In the cat training world, reinforcement is sometimes used incorrectly to indicate punishment. However, punishment carries nothing positive. It only instills fear in your cat, which can ultimately lead to unhealthy behaviors. Reinforcement is the opposite of punishment. It's something that enhances or increases healthy behaviors and favorable actions. Reinforcement can occur naturally in a cat, or it can be deliberately created by the owner. You create reinforcement through treats and verbal encouragement, but a cat can experience it through positive vibes, emotions, and of course, an opportunity to eat his favorite snack. The whole purpose of positive reinforcement is that the more often you encourage certain behavior, your cat's more likely to repeat it again. The best thing about this training method is that you can also apply it to your adult cat.

Positive reinforcement in a cat can also occur when he accidentally does something which results in more food or other things he loves. For example, if a cat keeps jumping and pulling stuff from the kitchen counter and accidentally pulls food on the ground, positive reinforcement just happened. He takes it as a message that when he jumps next time, the same thing will happen. That's why cat owners need to prevent positive reinforcement as much as introduce it. You need to make sure the environment isn't distractive or that it won't lead to scenarios described above. It's important to mention that although food is the first thing that comes to mind when positive reinforcement is involved, the method can also include some activity your cat loves, such as access to a desired area, verbal praise or more play and exercise.

Setting Up Sleeping Rules

Do you hear a flutter of cat paws across the floor all night, pouncing, scratching, and meowing? If you sleep lightly, you may notice that your cat's activity level increases during the night. While some British Shortahirs are more active at night than others, this is unsurprising given that cats are naturally nocturnal animals, meaning they prefer to sleep during the day and hunt at night.

Just because your cat is domesticated and has easy access to food doesn't mean their sleeping habits will change when you bring them home. Their natural proclivity for nighttime activity may take over and you may still hear galloping throughout the night. It takes time to gradually change her schedule and shift play time away from late at night or for you to learn to live with your nocturnal cat's behavior.

Here are some suggestions to assist you both:

Changing the Play Time to Day Time

If your cat is sleeping during the day, gently wake them up and encourage play. You can play with your cat before going to bed or throughout the day or, if safe, you may allow them to go outside during the day to stimulate their brain.

You can use interactive toys to pique their interest and keep them awake during the day, especially if you are not home to play with her.

Ignore the nighttime behaviors as much as possible. Giving a response will provide your cat with the engagement they seek, and they will want to play even more.

Keeping the Bedroom Clean and Quiet

Although changing the behavior is your first option, living with your cat necessitates some compromise. The change in play schedule may take some time and patience, so you may need to change some of your habits as well.

- Set the tone that the bedroom is a no-play zone by keeping all cat toys out.
- Of course, cats may decide that rolled-up socks and paper scraps are

also entertaining, so store any other potential toys as well.

- While sleeping, keep the bedroom door closed.
- Make a separate area or room for play to prevent commotion in your bedroom.

Because night activity is a natural instinct in cats, some felines may take some time to adjust, whereas others change their habits quickly. Be patient with your cat, and both of you will be much happier in the long run. Saying that, I have noticed with British Shorthair both adult and young cats that they are usually more active at first sunlight and tend to behave well throughout the night.

Cat Free Zones

Positive reinforcement will help your cat get what they need[1] – but only in the way you want them to. Along with positive reinforcement, you'll probably also need remote control training tools (also called adverse training) to enforce no-go areas. Spraying hot pepper sauce on the electrical lines your cat enjoys chewing or placing a blanket or foil over the couch corner your cat uses as a scratching post are two examples. This might seem negative, but it's a kind of training your cat won't connect with their owner. With time and patience you should be able to train your cat to respect your no-go areas and live in harmony with you. To begin, seek for obvious causes. Consider a cat who has just started urinating on the bed despite having a clean litter box. Is your cat suffering from a urinary tract infection or bladder stones? If your cat is sleeping on top of a basket of clean, dryer-warmed laundry, they could be cold or have arthritis. Before you go to the trouble of establishing no-go zones, make sure your cat isn't trying to tell you something and contact your vet if necessary. If your generally well-behaved cat is dragging defrosting steaks off the kitchen counter, defrost them somewhere else. Make a commitment to keep your litter box clean if your cat continues to reject it. Give your cat alternatives, also known as redirection. For example, cats scratch things to expend energy, identify their territory, and groom their claws, so trim your cat's claws and provide them with their own scratching posts made of carpet or sisal. You might also want to look into obtaining kitten nail caps (also known as claw caps). These brightly coloured plastic sleeves go over your cat's claws and prevent damage when they scratch. British Shorthairs are not normally climbers, but some young kittens might decide to scale curtains like catnip Kilimanjaro. More playtime, tall cat trees and kitten posts could be the answer for these adrenaline junkies. If you don't want your cat to spend their days dozing off on your laptop, give them alternative warm places to sleep. Consider placing multi-level cat trees or beds in sunny positions or warm, quiet areas. Remember: No-go areas must be no-go areas at all times[2]. Water spray, loud noises, and other aversive training tools can also be used. Suppose your cat won't stay off your desk or keeps cruising the counters. In that case, it's time to pull out your averse training toolkit, which includes unpleasant smells and tastes, unpleasant textures, and surprises like loud noises or water.

Bad odors such as cologne, perfume, or citrus scents. Some cats simply do not like strong odors, so use their natural aversion to help your no-cat zone cause. Squeeze a little lemon or orange zest on these spots, or sprinkle coarsely chopped citrus around the area to help keep your feline friend from scratching the couch or jumping on counters. You can also soak a few cotton balls in something strong-smelling, poke holes in a margarine container, and place it somewhere you don't want your rascal to be. Use caution when using strong-smelling deterrents; some citrus oil extracts, for example, can be fatal to cats.

Bad odors, such as hot sauce or one of the nontoxic sprays or ointments available at pet supply stores. To keep your angel's pearly whites where they belong, on the food, catnip, and toys, and away from electric cords and other no-nos, dab these areas with hot sauce, peppermint oil (not extract), or bitter apple. Because your cat's senses are acute, you won't need to use much.

Unappealing textures such as a nubby vinyl carpet runner, duct tape, rocks, sticky-backed shelf paper, aluminum foil, or anything else that will irritate your cat's paws.

IMPORTANT: Never spray water on your cat's face or ears. If you have a nervous cat, unwanted behaviour isn't best deterred by surprises. A fearful cat may avoid not only your no-go zones, but the entire house.

Training Your British Shorthair

Cats, it turns out, have a brain structure similar to other intelligent animals, including humans. It may surprise you to learn that your cat's brain structure is approximately 90% similar to yours. According to Psychology Today, a cat's cerebral cortex, responsible for rational decision-making and complex problem solving, contains approximately 300 million neurons. The cerebral cortex is involved in action planning, the overall interpretation of language, and storage of both short- and long-term memory, which is why your cat prefers to learn by doing rather than seeing. Not only that, but cats have more nerve cells in their visual areas of the brain than humans and the majority of other mammals. However, calculating how intelligent cats are is dependent on how intelligence is measured in the first place. British Shorthairs are extremely highly trainable social breeds who thrive when interacting and playing with their owners. With patience and persistence they can even be trained to do amazing tricks.

Clicker Training

This involves training your cat to come to you when they hear the sound of the clicker (or any other sound). You must use treats your cat really likes whenever you are training. Before you begin you must associate the sound of the clicker with something tasty. We don't want to move on to a full degree without a diploma first so before further training starts simply click the clicker and give your cat a treat and lots of praise. After doing this a few times your cat will start connecting the dots: "clicker = tasty food!". In a short period of time you should be able to increase the distance too and watch your cat come running. You can also train your cat to associate their names with something tasty or verbal praise. The same can be done if you want to teach your cat to sit. Use the clicker to get their attention, say sit while holding a tasty treat above their head. This will usually cause your cat to sit and look up, give them the treat when they do with verbal praise. You can also use hand signals after they learn the verbal command: Use your hand command after saying "sit". Once your cat is reliability following your hand signal you can then remove the verbal command and the clicker.

Harness Training

This training enables you to enjoy nice time together outdoors without worrying that your cat might run off in the wrong direction. Ensure your cat is fully vaccinated before doing this. Another thing to watch out for are dogs. Ask: is this a popular dog walker's area? If so you might want take things slowly and start with very short and safer distances.

Many people make the mistake of immediately putting the harness on the cat and dragging them around by the lead. You must let the cat get used to the harness before attempting to put it on them. Here is what to do:

- Purchase a harness (check for appropriate size first) and allow your cat to see and sniff it.
- Put the harness on for a short period and give your cat a treat and verbal praise. Allow your cat to dragit around the house under supervision.
- After your cat is comfortable with the harness and dragging the leash around the house, you can then start holding the leash and following them. Only apply slight restraint to allow them to slowly get used to you being in control.
- The next step is to take your cat outside (maybe around the garden) for a very short walk.

- Pick a quiet time of the day and an area where there is not a lot of traffic or barking dogs so you can both have an nice time outside.

Although you can teach your cat many tricks such as high five, sit, handshake, fetch, close doors to name a few training must always be done with patience and kindness (sometimes this might even become a two way learning endeavor). Start with short sessions and increase time slowly as your companion adapts to the new routine.

Are cats smarter than dogs?

The debate over whether cats or dogs are smarter is an ongoing one among cat and dog owners. Both sides appear to have valid reasons for believing their pet is the smartest, but what does the science actually say? According to animal intelligence research, dogs are generally regarded as the smarter of the two due to their greater trainability. Dogs have been domesticated for longer than cats. They appear to be more sociable and willing to please humans, which is why they have been successful in various tasks such as guiding the blind, search and rescue, and police work. However, this is only one method of assessing intelligence. Cats are thought to be more intelligent than dogs because they refuse to follow humans and participate in studies. They have their own minds and refuse to participate in meaningless tasks just to please their owners. Furthermore, while many people believe that cats ignore them because they don't understand them, the truth is that cats don't feel the same need to acknowledge them as dogs do. "Dogs come when they're called; cats take a message and get back to you," said Literature Professor Mary Bly. Studies on both cats and dogs provide more information about which is smarter. According to a 2009 study, cats are not as good as dogs or fish at counting or identifying quantities of things[3]. Another study discovered that cats can follow puzzles[4]. Still, unlike dogs, who will seek assistance from their owners, cats will simply keep trying until they get it. So, while dogs are unquestionably the more social of the two and are more likely to want to please their owners, cats are far more independent and prefer to do things on their own. This essentially means that the intelligence of a cat cannot be directly compared to that of a dog.

CHAPTER 15

SHOWING YOUR CAT

If you acquired a kitten from a breeder, you probably got an excellent pet with show potential. Your kitten can begin to show once he has reached the age of four months; however, you should be mindful that his immune system may not be as developed as other older show cats, making him more susceptible to sickness on the day. Before purchase, however, it's important to decide whether you would like to show your cat. This requires commitment and dedication to grooming and training from a young age. Your cat will need a calm and friendly disposition and knowing how to show your cat is the first step to training a champion. If your cat is easily scared or very shy, a cat show might not be the best choice. However, if your cat is okay with noise, new people, crowds, and a lot of other cats, you just might be able to win a prize. These shows should be enjoyed by the cats as well as their owners.

First Steps to Showing Your Cat

Attende a show. Going to a cat show for the aim of watching and learning is the best method to learn how to showcase your cat. You'll get a sense of how the show operates and how cats are assessed. Attending a competition as a spectator will help you feel more at ease in the situation, and you may even pick up some pointers from expert handlers. For health reasons, never touch (or help) a cat when you go to a cat show.

Pay attention to your cat's health. If you want your cat to be a viable contender, you must groom it properly. Make sure your cat is well-groomed, with clean ears and eyes, cut claws, and all of their immunizations up to date. Don't forget to take your up to date vet card with you and any other relevant documents. The GCCF (UK) emphasizes that contenders must ensure that the vaccination certificate has the name of your cat on it, and this must correspond with the show entry. It is best to put both the pedigree name and pet name in the certificate and vaccination certificate must describe the cat correctly: it should show the cat's full name, its correct breed, colour, sex and age. If it has the breeder's name and address on it you should add your own name and address. It's also critical to note that going to a show requires your cat to be healthy and fit. No fleas, no ear mites, no runny eyes, no bare or scabby patches of skin, no snuffles and sneezes[1].

Decide what show you're going to compete in. Cat shows are run by different organizations, and sometimes they'll require you to become a member before you can enter your cat. One other thing you can do to help your cat prepare for a show is to have friends and family members pick them up and get them used to being around people they're not familiar with. If your cat is already okay with this, gradually have your guests feel their paws and tail and try to open their mouth, as this is what judges will do during their examination. Exposing them to new situations will help your cat perform at their best during the show.

Find out about the details. A good top opening pet carrier to take to the show is essential. There is a strong chance that you will also need a clean plain white blanket, a non tip water bowl, a feeding bowl and litter tray - all white, although the litter itself need not be white.Wipe out the pen with a cloth; you can use a disinfectant for cats on the cloth, but do not spray the pen. If the show requires your cat to wear a tally, you will also need a piece of white tape or fine elastic to put it round its neck. It is extremely important to get your cat used to this before the show[2]. So practice is important.

Future Champion Training Checklist

Raising a champion is all about training! Below is a list of kitten training needs to be implemented well before a show.

- ☐ Safely show your kitten how to play with toys in unfamiliar areas such as on your desk, in your lap, on a grooming table.
- ☐ Teach your kitten how to jump up for the toy, trusting you.
- ☐ Begin kitten baths and bathe every 3 weeks, then 2 weeks as you get closer to showing and then weekly - one month before the kitten goes to his fist cat show.
- ☐ Share loud noises near your kitten.
- ☐ Get the kitten comfortable with having its paws, tail touched and mouth opened by new people.
- ☐ Introduce your kitten to family and friends.
- ☐ Have your kitten learn to be carried on your hand and forearm.

- [ ] Teach your kitten how to use and enjoy a scratching post.
- [ ] Commend your kitten with praise and reward your kitten after training sessions.

The Show

The judging should begin about 10 a.m., depending on the show, but the general audience is usually admitted in the middle of the day until about 5 p.m. It is recommended that contestants arrive two hours early to locate their cat's pen and settle in. You should have enough time to brush and feed your cat, but you must remove the bowl before judging, leaving only the water bowl within the pen, and save the best blanket for last, or there is a chance you will find it covered by the contents of the litter box.

You and your cat may be assigned a number, which will correspond to the pen on the judging table where you will place your cat. Take your cat to their pen and sit in the correct location for handlers when your number is called. Following that, you must wait for the judges' decision. The judges and their stewards walk around the hall, taking the cats out of their pens one by one; you can spot them by their badges and white coats. Judges normally do not speak to exhibitors or the general audience until they have completed their judging. The results are written in a book, and slips from the books emerge on the results board later in the day; the boards will be surrounded by exhibitors who are eagerly looking for their cats' placements.

The pens are usually arranged in rows, starting with the Persians in pen #1 and concluding with the Siamese in pen #10. It's possible that the non-pedigree cats are in a separate portion of the hall. The show should feature a booklet with information about the cats, their breeds, and colors, as well as adverts placed by breeders, which will be quite useful if you are considering purchasing a kitten. Many shows contain posters or leaflets to assist you in navigating the venue.

Make sure your cat is comfy when you return home after the show. If possible without disturbing the cat, avoid allowing all of your cats to interact with the show cat for a few days until any risk of infection has passed. Cat shows may be a delightful experience for any inquisitive cat, as well as a terrific way for you and your feline companion to bond. Consider the first show to be a warm-up, and if it goes well, you could be on your road to becoming Grand Champion[3].

Things You Should Consider

Cats should be introduced to exhibiting when they are kittens so that they can become accustomed to the concept before becoming too set in their ways. Also, although great precautions are taken during shows to decrease the risk of infection, there is always a small chance that your beloved companion could become unwell thereafter. The question you need to ask yourself is: Is it worth it? If you have a pedigree cat, you must decide whether or not your cat is good enough to be shown. Look for the TICA standards online[4] and seek guidance from the breeder and any other knowledgeable individuals you know. If you don't know anyone, contact the GCCF (UK) or the American Cat Fanciers Association and chat to them. They might even refer you to a club you can join so you can start making friends with individuals who exhibit cats.

The Judging Process

Cat shows are not the same as the dog shows you see on TV. Cat handlers sit in the crowd and aren't part of the judging as this is absolutely objective. Cats are placed in pens with numbers allocated to them, and the judge inspects each one according to the breed standard. The winner is then decided, and the winning cat advances to the finals.

CHAPTER 16

SENIOR MOMENTS

Due to the advance of veterinarian care, nutrition improvements and better care knowledge our companions are often able to enjoy longer and healthier lives. It's important to notice that not all cats age the same way. It's helpful, however, to be aware of signs that might affect your British Shorthair as they start entering their senior years at around 11 years of age.

Aging Signs

Less Acute Senses

You might notice subtle signs that your cat isn't hearing or seeing as well as it used to. Do not allow your cat outside if you notice vision or hearing loss. Your cat might also start eating less due to a lack in their ability to smell and taste, so changing an older cat's diet may be necessary. Consult your veterinarian first to avoid giving a senior cat anything that will cause an upset tummy. You can also try slightly warming your pet's existing wet food to improve the smell, but be careful not to overheat it.

Blind Cats Checklist

- ☐ Try to maintain your home routine and avoid moving furniture.
- ☐ New objects and smells will need to be introduced gradually.
- ☐ Don't stop playing with your cat. Crinkly and catnip-stuffed toys can still be great fun.
- ☐ Do not cut your cat's whiskers as they are vital for orientation.
- ☐ If you pick up a blind cat and move her, place her somewhere she can

orient herself

Physiological Changes

As your cat gets older you might notice physical problems that affect us humans such as arthritis, stiffness and inability to control their bladder and bowels. Visits to the litter box may become more frequent, which might need to be changed to a lower tray to allow easier access. Also, due to their age your elderly cat might not feel as confident going outside as they used to. It's normal for cats to lose muscle mass as they age but always have any extreme changes in weight, both losses and gains evaluated by your veterinarian. It is also advisable to keep an eye on your cat's coat as it might need help with more frequent brushing and pay attention to any thinning or matting as both could be signs of potential bad health. Claw clipping may also become more necessary as they cannot be easily retracted in the elderly cat. Be ready to help with the cleaning of personal areas as arthritis can stop access to those hard spots. A warm washcloth and plain, clean water should do the job just fine. You might as well consider providing bed, food, water and litter in reasonable proximity so that they are easily accessible.

NOTE: Due to stiffness the elderly cat will also groom less, especially towards the base of their spine. Senior cats benefit greatly from combing and brushing from their owners.

Behavioural Changes

According to a survey, 66% of senior cats use more sounds to get food and attention and 81% become more sociable, loving and affectionate[1]. Some cats may develop harsh vocalization at night around the age of 10 and fifteen, perhaps due to deafness or short-term memory loss, stopping only when they receive reassurance from their owners[2]. Night-time vocalization can also be linked to hyperthyroidism, a condition often seen in elderly cats. This condition causes increased heart and respiration rates, increased appetite and weight loss.

It's also very important to be aware of subtle changes in mood and behavior when dealing with an elderly cat for health reasons. British Shorthairs are very relaxed and spend a lot of time curled up snoozing, usually eighteen hours a day or more. This type of normal slowing down may be difficult to distinguish from actual illness. Cats are great at hiding their pain and illness so use your best judgment and knowledge of your pet's personality. Book a vet visit if not sure.

How To Make Your Elderly Cat More Comfortable

Regular Checkups. Seniors are more likely to develop dental issues, and all skin growths should be thoroughly checked. Changes in litter box habits should be monitored, keep an eye out for urinary tract infection or kidney problems. If the cat is vomiting more than usual, a vet visit may be in order. Due to a weaker immune system your senior British Shorthair might need a vet visit every 6 months. Is your cat drinking large amounts of water? This might indicate the presence of diabetes. Aging cats can also suffer from hyperthyroidism and high blood pressure, both of which are treatable. The most common problems affecting elderly cats are: arthritis, chronic renal failure, deafness, blindness, hyperthyroidism, bronchitis and dental problems.

No wild play. According to research 10% of senior cats play regularly, 48% play occasionally and 15% stopped playing completely[3]. Soft play should be encouraged and children will need to learn how to play gently with your senior cat as they will have less energy than when they were younger.

Milder exercise. Even senior cats will enjoy milder games and shorter walks to keep them healthier.

Senior food. Although given in smaller quantities, high quality protein based food is essential. Many good brands now make food specially formulated for our senior friends.

Warm bed. Because older cats sleep more, they are more prone to be cold. Provide your senior cat with a clean warm bed and lots of quiet time in a draft free area. The warmth will also help if your pet is suffering from arthritis. Sometimes a warm bed inside a cardboard box may provide a simple yet effective (and more protected) solution for your senior friend.

Parasite free. Check for biting bugs often as this is the last thing your senior cat will want to deal with.

Plenty of fresh water. Keep your cat hydrated. This will help with energy levels and digestion and help with joint stiffness.

Prioritise accessibility. An older cat may not jump up to the window sill, but they may still want to bask in the sun. Allow your cat access to their favourite places without having to jump.

More love. A total of 97% of people say that their cat is as much pleasure when they get older as they were when younger, giving a lot more for a lot less[4]. Almost without exception, the senior cat will turn to you for love and attention in their old age. Your now senior companion will rely on your love, attention and require more patience to see them through their aging years.

Saying Goodbye

Saying goodbye to a longtime friend is both heartbreaking and a great act of love. Euthanasia is a difficult topic to discuss. Do not listen to anyone who puts you under pressure to make this difficult decision. Only your cat can tell you when it's time to say goodbye. At the same time it's important to do our best to look at our friend's situation from a logical point of view to prevent further pain and suffering. Helpful questions to ask are: is my cat suffering from extreme old age? Is this an incurable illness that is causing them much pain? Is this a serious injury?

Here is a quick checklist of what to do:

- ☐ Get the most recent medical information.
- ☐ Do your own research.
- ☐ Keep a daily log.
- ☐ Spend extra time with your cat.
- ☐ Plan ahead and have an idea of what you wish to make at the end: burial, cremation, return of ashes, memorial.
- ☐ Accept help from family and friends.

Euthanasia

This procedure can be done either at home or at the vet. Prices range from £30 - £300 ($40 - $400) depending on the vet. A good veterinarian will have a good relationship with both you and your cat and will help you through this difficult stage. Euthanasia is usually a two-step process:

1. The veterinarian will inject the cat with a sedative in order to make them sleepy and comfortable.
2. The veterinarian will then inject a special drug that will peacefully stop their heart. The cat will not experience any awareness whatsoever and the experience is similar to a human falling asleep under anaesthesia. This peaceful step will take about 10 to 20 seconds. The vet will then ensure that the cat's heart has stopped.

After Passing

You may feel depressed, teary and sad and find it hard to focus or concentrate after the death of your beloved friend. Mainly if it forms a link with a partner that has passed away or the memories of happier times. Allow yourself grieving time and understand that recovering from grief does not mean that you forget about your cat or love them any less. You may need to speak to other cat or animal lovers who understand your loss. Sometimes a simple, "I am so sorry you lost your friend." is all we need to hear in times like these as even when we are not at our best, our pets still show us unconditional love and this should not be minimised. Also, considering the acquisition of another companion is not disrespectful to the memory of the departed one, but a compliment.

The Rainbow Bridge poem below has given solace to many when grieving the loss of a fur friend.

Just this side of heaven is a place called Rainbow Bridge.

When an animal dies that has been especially close to someone here, that pet goes to Rainbow Bridge.

There are meadows and hills for all of our special friends so they can run and play together.

There is plenty of food, water and sunshine, and our friends are warm and comfortable.

All the animals who had been ill and old are restored to health and vigor. Those who were hurt or maimed are made whole and strong again, just as we remember them in our dreams of days and times gone by.

The animals are happy and content, except for one small thing; they each miss someone very special to them, who had to be left behind.

They all run and play together, but the day comes when one suddenly stops and looks into the distance. His bright eyes are intent. His eager body quivers.

Suddenly he begins to run from the group, flying over the green grass, his legs carrying him faster and faster.

You have been spotted, and when you and your special friend finally meet, you cling together in joyous reunion, never to be parted again. The happy kisses rain upon your face; your hands again caress the beloved head, and you look once more into the trusting eyes of your pet, so long gone from your life but never absent from your heart.

Then you cross Rainbow Bridge together....

- *(Author unknown)*

Memorials

You can honour the passing of a beloved companion in many ways. You can have your pet cremated and preserve their ashes in a special urn in a place of honour or sprinkle their ashes under a favourite tree or special place. Paintings and photos with engraved Rainbow Poems or wooden plaques are also suitable ways to keep their memory close. You can also create a forever place online to remember precious memories forever, see www.muffinandpoppy.co.uk/memorials.

Should You Adopt A Senior Cat?

Many lovely older pets are put down every year when all they need is a loving home. Saying that, you will need to be aware that you will be taking in a furball with established habits, preferences and pre-existing needs. Still, a loving relationship with an older cat in its golden years might still be possible.

If you are prepared to meet the special needs of a senior cat, including late-in-life veterinary expenses, giving an older, homeless cat home is a vital part of feline rescue work. This is an area of that mission that always needs more willing volunteers.

CHAPTER 17

Cats And Babies

If you're having a child, you might be worried about how to introduce your beloved British Shorthair to the new member of the family. The good news are that cats and babies can coexist happily, but it will take some planning to ensure that everything runs smoothly. Much like preparing your home for the arrival of a new baby, it is critical to begin preparing your cat for the upcoming changes as soon as you can. You and your cat will be protected from stress and undesired behavioural difficulties (such as spraying) if you plan ahead of time, allowing the entire family to live well together.

How to Get Ready Before the Baby Arrives

While it may seem daunting, there are a few things you can add to your baby's to-do list to assist your cat adjust to sharing their home with a new baby. First and foremost, take precautions for your health. You've probably heard of toxoplasmosis if you own a cat. Toxoplasmosis is caused by a parasite that can be transmitted from cats to humans. It can also be passed from mother to unborn child. This parasite causes various health issues in an unborn baby, including blindness, deafness, and hydrocephalus. Avoid stray cats and keep your cat indoors to prevent the spread of this parasite from cat to human. When working with litter boxes or outdoor gardens, always wear gloves. It is best for pregnant cat owners to avoid scooping litter as much as possible and to have regular screenings. Secondly, make gradual adjustments. As you prepare your home for your new baby, make time to spend with your cat, preparing them for life with a baby. Take the following steps to assist your cat in adjusting smoothly:

Environmental Adjustments

Make your cat familiar with baby sounds by playing recordings of babies gurgling, cooing and even screaming throughout the day in the months leading up to your baby's birth. Begin quietly and gradually increase the volume as your cat becomes accustomed to the new sounds. To avoid causing stress to your cat, go slowly through the process. A newborn and new baby objects can aggravate your cat's senses because cats rely largely on smell. Therefore, it's important to make your cat familiar with baby scents to help your fluff ball to acclimate before the baby arrives. Bring in powders, shampoos, and formula. When you use baby items on your own skin, you can help your cat form pleasant associations with new odours.

Interaction Adjustments

British Shorthairs are extremely calm and warm and enjoy being petted, but in rare cases you might find unneutered cats that do not. You must prepare your cat to be handled by a child by increasing the number of times your cat gets petted. You must also become more aware of its preferences concerning petting and when your baby grows more mobile, be ready to prevent the little one from upsetting your cat. If your cat is used to playing with your hands, put an end to it as soon as possible. It may also be a good idea to clip your cat's claws. Even a gentle teddy bear like the British Shorthair can accidentally upset or injure a baby. Teach your cat that only toys should be used for play. Hand games must be stopped and new games with toys must be introduced preferably well before your baby's arrival.

How to Introduce Your Baby to Your Kitten

Chances are you will be tired. Excited, but overwhelmingly tired. You're now embarking on a brand new routine so take the time to introduce your baby to your kitten. Allow your cat to reconnect with you and meet your baby safely and without interruption. Set aside some quiet time with just you, your baby and your kitten to meet each other peacefully. Taking the time to ensure that both the cat and the baby are safe and happy will result in a pleasant home. As you, your baby, and your cat get used to your new life together, be on the lookout for indications of stress. Take into account these two factors:

Your Cat's Curiosity

Place a baby blanket or piece of clothing in a quiet, safe location for your British Shorthair to explore at their leisure. This allows your cat to adjust to the baby at its own pace. It may take some time for your British Shorthair and baby to get along. Be patient and keep in mind that, in the beginning, your cat may prefer to avoid the baby.

With a newborn in the house, keeping your cat clean and pest-free is more important than ever. Keep your cat indoors, maintain regular screenings with your veterinarian and stay on top of preventative prescriptions such as dewormer and deflea treatments. Keep in mind that dirty nappies (diapers) may encourage your cat to make their own mess. Always dispose of them in their proper sealed containers as soon as possible. Also, by now you already know that your cat enjoys snuggling, but this can be dangerous since newborns cannot move their heads. When you can't immediately supervise your child and cat together, keep the bedroom door closed. Even if your cat and baby become acquainted, you must not leave them alone together. Provide a quiet, safe location where your cat can be separated from your baby if necessary.

CHAPTER 18

FAQs About Your Cat

Have you ever wondered why cats purr, why they knead, or why they are so fond of boxes? If this is the case, you are not alone. At the time of writing, according to Google, the following are the ten most frequently asked questions about cats:

What causes cats to purr?

Purring is typically associated with an enjoyable activity, such as nursing, being pet, grooming another cat, or simply being in a comfortable environment. Still, cats also purr when they are sick, injured, or stressed. This may serve to soothe them, but researchers have discovered that purring actually helps them heal due to the low frequency of the vibrations[1]. Some behaviorists believe that purring can also be used to communicate, such as when kittens communicate with their mother or when they are hungry (which is often combined with a meow).

What is the average lifespan of a cat?

Outdoor cats have a life expectancy of 2 to 5 years, whereas indoor cats have a life expectancy of 15 to 20 years. This is because outdoor cats face far more dangers than indoor cats, such as being hit by a vehicle, encounters with other wild animals, ingesting a poison, food availability, various diseases and parasites, and exposure to the elements. Other factors that influence their longevity include preventative care, nutrition, and lifestyle. Being overweight or obese, for example, can reduce a person's lifespan by more than two years.

What is the purpose of kneading in cats?

Kittens knead on their mothers while nursing stimulates milk production. They frequently continue to do so as adults when they are content or want attention. Others believe it has something to do with preparing their bed for sleep or marking their territory with the scent glands in their paws.

What causes cats to sleep so much?

Cats can sleep for up to 16 hours per day in short bursts that alternate between dozing and deep sleep. Some cats, particularly senior cats, can sleep for up to 20 hours per day. They sleep so much because they are predators who expend a lot of energy in short bursts when hunting. They're also crepuscular, which means they're most active at dawn and dusk, so you'll probably see them sleeping during the day.

What is the purpose of a cat's whiskers?

Whiskers, also known as vibrissae, are very sensitive tactile hairs that connect to a cat's muscular system and nervous system and provide a lot of information about its environment, particularly its position in space (such as whether they can fit through a tight space), distance, or air currents. Still, they are especially useful in low light or darkness. They can also be used to communicate with one another. When they are scared or threatened, they will pull them against their face, pointing them forward when they are excited. Never cut or pluck a cat's whiskers!

What effect does catnip have on cats?

Catnip is a mint-family herb, and whether or not a cat responds to it is determined by genetics. Surprisingly, only about half of all cats have this gene. Researchers believe that the smell of catnip activates receptors in the brain that make cats happy. Eating it, on the other hand, has the effect of calming them down. If your cat enjoys catnip, you can used it as a training tool when teaching your cat to use a scratching post or encouraging them to play more. NOTE: While cats are unlikely to overdose on catnip, too much of it can make them sick.

Why do cats despise water?

Water is unappealing to many cats for a variety of reasons. Most cats have had very few experiences with water, for starters, and they are frequently negative (e.g. bath). In fact, because they evolved in desert climates, they have never been particularly fond of water. Their fur is also not designed to repel water, making it uncomfortable if it gets wet. However, not all cats despise water. Certain cat breeds, such as Abyssinians, Turkish Vans, Bengals, and Maine Coons, enjoy swimming.

What is the purpose of cats eating grass?

Because grass contains much fiber, most veterinarians believe cats eat it to relieve gastrointestinal issues or get rid of parasites. It also contains nutrients such as folic acid which helps with the production of hemoglobin (a red protein responsible for transporting oxygen in the blood). Other cats, on the other hand, may simply enjoy the taste of it. Just make sure your cat isn't eating any toxic plants or chemically treated grass. If you notice them eating a lot of grass, consult your vet because there could be an underlying problem.

What is it about boxes that cats find appealing?

Cats enjoy boxes because they provide a sense of security. In the wild, places like this keep predators from seeing them or sneaking up on them. It can also come in handy when stalking prey. Boxes are useful in stressful situations because cats associate small spaces like this with safety. They also provide a warm, cozy sleeping environment for them. A great way to give your cat a box and help them overcome their fear of the carrier is to leave the carrier somewhere in your home where your cat spends a lot of time, open the door or take it off, and place bedding inside for them.

What is the name of a group of cats?

A clowder is a group of cats. It can also be called a glaring, particularly if the cats are uncertain of each other. A litter of kittens can also be called a kindle.

What is a lover of cats called?

Ailurophile is the term used for cat lovers.

Why does my cat pick up food and drop it on the floor to eat it?

Is your cat's bowl too small? Some cats do not like the feeling of their whiskers touching the side of their food bowl. This potential sensitivity is called whiskers stress and the best thing to do is to switch to a bowl that is more like a tray. Is your cat sharing the bowl with other cats? It might be that the bowl area is too crowded and your cat is just looking for a more comfortable area to eat.

Are there natural remedies for common problems?

These are some natural solutions I've used successfully in the past.

Bicarb. Used to clean dirty and remove smells. It also seems to cause cats to avoid soiling in the treated area.

Oats. Is your cat constipated? Add a little bit of oats to their wet food.

Onion. So, you have a smell problem because of your cat? Or maybe a particular room or corridor smell a little sour and you want a natural solution. Onions are natural air fresheners. Cut an onion in half and place it in the affected area. The area might smell like onion in the first couple of days but wait for the onion to do its thing. The place will have fresh air again for 2-3 weeks.

Extra Virgin Olive Oil. Use the purest olive oil you can find. Great for fur problems. Had a problem with what looked like an allergy patch in the ear of one of our cats once that even our vet could not fix. Used a little pure olive oil and the problem disappeared for good.

Peppermint. Use highly diluted peppermint essential oil for cleaning purposes. Great to keep your cat's environment clean and bug free. Please note that peppermint is not good for cats in large quantities, so do keep peppermint plants or essential oils safely stored.

CONCLUSION

As a cat lover, I congratulate you and sincerely thank you for reading this book with heartfelt gratitude.

Cats are very majestic feline creatures that always seem to demand a lot of love. If you treat them right, they will become your best friend. The teddy bear-like British Shorthair even more so. I have, proudly, been a cat parent to gorgeous British Shorthair cats now for over a decade. I have had cats most of my life but have found the British Shorthair the ideal house companion if you prefer a breed that isn't always underfoot or in your face but happy to share their lives next to you. British Shorthairs prefer to remain low-key; they are affectionate but not clingy, playful but not overactive. They are quiet, even-tempered, and undemanding, with a touch of typical British reticence when first introduced. They become extremely loyal companions once they overcome their initial reluctance, however. These lovable companions require love and attention to develop into the loyal, loving companions they can be; the more attention and affection you give them, the more they will return in kind. British Shorthairs are confident and devoted once they get to know and trust you. They enjoy following you from room to room to keep an eye on your activities. They are calm, quiet companions who value quality time without demanding your undivided attention.

You might find your British Shorthair waiting for your arrival by the front door or running to greet you as you come home. British Shorthairs also make excellent apartment cats because they are alert and playful without being hyperactive or destructive. British Shorthairs are more likely to be loyal to their entire family than to a single person. They are more self-sufficient than many other breeds and usually adapt well to most situations.

British Shorthairs are not usually vocal cats; instead, they make tiny squeaking sounds rather than meows, which is quite amusing given their burly bodies. They compensate by having some of the loudest purrings you've ever heard; British Shorthairs are well-known for their motorboat purrs.

The regal British Shorthair, on the other hand, are not all lap cats. Some would rather sit next to you or curl up at your feet than snuggle on your lap. British Shorthairs dislike being picked up and will push you away with their legs stiffly stretched out. They, too, dislike being kissed, but head presses are acceptable, and they accept petting (except on their tummies) with gusto and mighty purrs of appreciation. As long as proper introductions are made, they get along with other animals in the house, including dogs. British Shorthairs are excellent with children, and children adore these plush, smiling companions.

I wish you the best of luck on your journey with your new teddy bear companion.

Eric De Souza

=^.^=

APPENDIX A

PLANTS POISONOUS TO CATS

It is very difficult to keep British Shorthairs from nibbling on plants as they love to explore their surroundings. Removing the plant from your home when in doubt is always a good guideline. Also If a plant is poisonous, assume all parts of the plant are poisonous. The list below is a fairly comprehensive though not exhaustive list. These are plants poisonous to cats that must be avoided if there are cats in your home. Please <u>note that lilies</u>*, in particular, are dangerous to cats. While in some cases, just parts of a plant (bark, leaves, seeds, berries, roots, tubers, spouts, green shells) might be poisonous, this list rules out the whole plant. If you must have any of them, keep them safely out of your British Shorthair reach. Should your cat eat part of a poisonous plant, rush your cat to your veterinarian as soon as possible. If you can, take the plant with you for ease of identification.

Almond (Pits of)
Aloe Vera
Alocasia
Amaryllis
Apple (seeds)
Apple Leaf
Croton
Apricot (Pits of)
Arrowgrass
Asparagus Fern
Autumn Crocus
Avocado (fuit and pit)
Azalea Baby's
Breath
Baneberry
Bayonet
Beargrass
Beech
Belladonna
Bird of Paradise
Bittersweet
Black-eyed

Susan
Black Locust
Bleeding Heart
Bloodroot
Bluebonnet
Box
Boxwood
Branching Ivy
Buckeyes
Buddist Pine
Burning Bush
Buttercup Cactus
Candelabra
Caladium
Calla Lily
Castor Bean
Ceriman
Charming
Dieffenbachia
Cherry (pits, seeds & wilting
Cherry, most wild
varieties

Cherry, ground
Cherry, Laurel
Chinaberry
Chinese
Evergreen
Christmas Rose
Chrysanthemum
Cineria
Clematis
Cordatum
Coriaria
Cornflower
Corn Plant
Cornstalk Plant
Croton
Corydalis
Crocus, Autumn
Crown of Thorns
Cuban Laurel
Cutleaf
Philodendron
Cycads
Cyclamen

145

Daffodil	**Hellebore**	**Breadfruit**
Daphne	Hemlock, Poison	Miniature Croton
Datura	**Hemlock, Water**	**Mistletoe**
Deadly	Henbane	Mock Orange
Nightshade	**Holly**	**Monkshood**
Death Camas	Horsebeans	Moonseed
Devil's Ivy	**Horsebrush**	**Morning Glory**
Delphinium	Hellebore	Mother-in Law's
Decentrea	**Horse Chestnuts**	Tongue
Dieffenbachia	Hurricane Plant	**Morning Glory**
Dracaena Palm	**Hyacinth**	Mountain Laurel
Dragon Tree	Hydrangea	**Mushrooms**
Dumb Cane	**Indian Rubber**	Narcissus
Easter Lily *	**Plant**	**Needlepoint Ivy**
Eggplant	Indian Tobacco	Nephytis
Elaine	**Iris**	**Nightshade**
Elderberry	Iris Ivy	**Oleander**
Elephant Ear	**Jack in the**	Onion
Emerald Feather	**Pulpit**	**Oriental Lily ***
English Ivy	Janet Craig	Peace Lily
Eucalyptus	Dracaena	**Peach (pits and**
Euonymus	**Japanese Show**	**wilting leaves)**
Evergreen Ferns	**Lily ***	Pencil Cactus
Fiddle-leaf fig	Java Beans	**Peony**
Florida Beauty	**Jessamine**	Periwinkle
Flax	Jerusalem Cherry	**Philodendron**
Four O'Clock	**Jimson Weed**	Pimpernel
Foxglove	Jonquil	**Plumosa Fern**
Fruit Salad Plant	**Jungle Trumpets**	Poinciana
Geranium	Kalanchoe	**Poinsettia (low**
German Ivy	**Lacy Tree**	**toxicity)**
Giant Dumb	**Philodendron**	Poison Hemlock
Cane	Lantana	**Poison Ivy**
Glacier Ivy	**Larkspur**	Poison Oak
Golden Chain	Laurel	**Pokeweed**
Gold	**Lily**	Poppy
Dieffenbachia	Lily Spider	**Potato**
Gold Dust	**Lily of the Valley**	Pothos
Dracaena	Locoweed	**Precatory Bean**
Golden Glow	**Lupine**	Primrose
Golden Pothos	Madagascar	**Privet, Common**
Gopher Purge	Dragon Tree	Red Emerald
Hahn's	**Marble Queen**	**Red Princess**
Self-Branching	Marigold	Red-Margined
Ivy	**Marijuana**	Dracaena
Heartland	Mescal Bean	**Rhododendron**
Philodendron	**Mexican**	Rhubarb

146

Ribbon Plant
Rosemary Pea
Rubber Plant
Saddle Leaf
Philodendron
Sago Palm
Satin Pothos
Schefflera
Scotch Broom
Silver Pothos
Skunk Cabbage
Snowdrops
Snow on the
Mountain
Spotted Dumb
Cane

Staggerweed
Star of
Bethlehem
String of Pearls
Striped
Dracaena
Sweetheart Ivy
Sweetpea
Swiss Cheese
plant
Tansy Mustard
Taro Vine
Tiger Lily *
Tobacco
Tomato Plant
(green fruit,

stem and leaves)
Tree
Philodendron
Tropic Snow
Dieffenbachia
Tulip
Tung Tree
Virginia Creeper
Water Hemlock
Weeping Fig
Wild Call
Wisteria Yews (e.g.
Japanese Yew)
English Yew
Western Yew
American Yew

APPENDIX B

FOODS HARMFUL TO CATS

Alcoholic beverages
Bones (fish, poultry, etc)
Canned tuna
Coffee and energy drinks
Chocolate
Citrus oil
Dairy products (some cats cannot break down the lactose)
Dog Food
Fat trimmings
Grapes and raisins
Garlic
Iron supplements
Liver
Macadamia nuts
Marijuana
Milk
Mushrooms
Onions
Persimmons
Potato
Raw eggs, raw meat and raw fish
Rhubarb
Salt
Sugar
Tea
Tobacco
Tomato leaves and stems
Yeast dough
Xylitol

APPENDIX C

A Balanced Home-Cooked Diet

The recipe below should produce approximately 800 calories, which is enough to feed a typical housecat for three days[1].

Lean chicken 140 g (5 oz)
Liver 30 g (1 oz)
Uncooked rice 70 g (2½ oz)
Sterilized bone meal 10 g (⅓ oz)
Iodized salt 2 g (a pinch)
Sunflower or corn oil 5 ml (1 tsp)

Preparation

1. Cook the rice, bone meal, salt and oil in twice the volume of water for 20 minutes.
2. Add the chicken and liver, simmering for another 10 minutes.
3. Blend thoroughly.

BIBLIOGRAPHY

Introduction
[1]https://www.gccfcats.org/getting-a-cat/choosing/cat-breeds/british/

Chapter 3
[1]https://feline-nutrition.org/features/a-brief-history-of-commercial-pet-food
[2]Justine S. Patrick, Deconstructing the Regulatory Façade: Why Confused Consumers Feed their Pets Ring Dings and Krispy Kremes, Digital Access to Scholarship at Harvard (DASH), April 2006.
[3]Vicky Halls, Cat Confidential, Bantam Books, 2004, p.275.

Chapter 7
[1]https://www.food.gov.uk/business-guidance/pet-food
[2]Dr. Bruce Fogle, Cat Owner's Manual, DK, 2003, p.202.
[3]https://www.vet.cornell.edu/departments-centers-and-institutes/cornell-feline-health-center/health-information/feline-health-topics/feeding-your-cat
[4]Lisa A. Pierson, DVM, California, https://catinfo.org/
[5]https://pets.webmd.com/cats/guide/cat-treats-and-snacks-whats-healthy #1
[6]Ibid.
[7]Ibid.
[8]https://pets.webmd.com/cats/guide/cat-treats-and-snacks-whats-healthy #2
[9]Dr. Bruce Fogle, Cat Owner's Manual, DK, 2003, p.204.

Chapter 10
[1]https://www.aaha.org/aaha-guidelines/preventive-healthcare/summary/
[2]https://www.aaha.org/globalassets/02-guidelines/preventive-healthcare/ felinepreventiveguidelines_ppph.pdf

Chapter 11
[1]https://www.gccfcats.org/breeding-cats/the-experienced-breeder/keeping-a-stud/
[2]https://www.britannica.com/science/estrus#ref5672
[3]ttps://www.sciencedirect.com/topics/medicine-and-dentistry/proestrus
[4]Dr. Bruce Fogle, Cat Owner's Manual, DK, 2003, p.143.
[5]https://www.gccfcats.org/wp-content/uploads/2021/12/

Kitten-Gestation.pdf
[6]Dr. Bruce Fogle, Cat Owner's Manual, DK, 2003, p.143..

Chapter 12
[1]https://www.investopedia.com/terms/p/pet-insurance.asp
[2]Ibid.
[3]https://www.petfirst.com/pet-fun/
a-short-history-of-pet-insurance-around-the-world/
[4]https://www.iii.org/fact-statistic/
facts-statistics-pet-ownership-and-insurance#:~:text=Sixty%2Dseven%20
percent%20of%20U.S.,year%20the%20survey%20was%20conducted.

Chapter 13
[1]https://www.humanesociety.org/resources/
travel-safely-your-pet-car-airplane-ship-or-train
[2]https://youtu.be/TZDW-NSK6Dc
[3]https://www.gov.uk/government/news/
new-rules-for-pet-travel-from-1-january-2021
[4]https://www.gov.uk/government/publications/
pet-travel-approved-air-sea-rail-and-charter-routes-for-the-movement-of-p
ets/approved-air-routes-for-pet-travel
[5]https://www.gov.uk/taking-your-pet-abroad
[6]https://www.iata.org/en/youandiata/travelers/traveling-with-pets/

Chapter 14
[1]Johnson, P. Twisted Whiskers: Solving Your Cat's Behavior Problems,
The Crossing Press, 1994.
[2]Johnson-Bennett, P. Think Like a Cat: How to Raise a Well-Adjusted Cat,
NOT a Sour Puss, Penguin Books, 2000.
[3]https://link.springer.com/article/10.1007/s10164-008-0121-0
[4]https://link.springer.com/article/10.1007/s10071-005-0008-1

Chapter 15
[1]https://www.gccfcats.org/shows
[2]Ibid
[3]https://www.gccfcats.org/Shows/Supreme-Show
[4]https://www.tica.org/breeds/
browse-all-breeds?view=article&id=829:british-shorthair-breed&catid=79
or download it from:
https://www.muffinandpoppy.co.uk/wp-content/
uploads/2022/01/bs.pdf

Chapter 16
[1]Vicky Halls, Cat Confidential, Bantam Books, 2004, p.281.
[2]Ibid, p.282
[3]Ibid, p.284
[4]Ibid, p.295

Chapter 18
[1]Fauna Communications Research Institute: "The Felid Purr: A bio-mechanical healing mechanism."
https://asa.scitation.org/doi/10.1121/1.4777098

Appendix C
[1]Dr. Bruce Fogle, Cat Owner's Manual, DK, 2003, p.202.

Glossary

A

Ailurophile - One who loves and is actively involved with cats. Also, a committed member of the cat fancy.

Ailurophobe - Any person who harbors a dislike of cats or who has a fear of cats. This can respond to a bad experience, a simple expression of preference, or an actual phobia.

Allergen - The primary allergen in cats is the protein Fel d 1, which is produced by the animal's saliva and sebaceous glands. In people with sensitivity, Fel d 1 triggers a pronounced allergic reaction.

Allergy - An allergy is a pronounced sensitivity to an environmental agent that triggers a cascade of responses in a sensitive person, including but not limited to sneezing, watering eyes, itching, and skin rashes.

Alter - An accepted term indicating that a cat or dog has been neutered or spayed and thus made incapable of reproduction. A similar, colloquial term frequently used with the same meaning is "fixed."

B

Bloodline - In pedigreed cats, the bloodline is the animal's verifiable line of descent. It is used to establish pedigree.

Breed Standard - Feline governing organizations publish established sets of standards that outline the points considered necessary for an individual animal to be regarded as a perfect example of any given breed. The standards are used to judge at cat shows.

Breed - Any group of cats with a defined set of physical characteristics that are reliably passed on to subsequent generations and that distinguish them from other types of cats is said to be a distinct "breed."

Breeder - A breeder is a person who works with male and female cats of a particular breed, pairing the animals to produce offspring that exhibit exceptionally high quality according to the accepted standards for the type of cat in question.

Breeding - In the sense of organized promulgation of a breed within the cat fancy, breeding is the process whereby sires and dams are paired with an eye toward the superior quality of their offspring.

Breeding Program - A breeding program is an organized effort to selectively breed superior individuals of any type of cat for the express purpose of producing offspring of exceptional quality.

Breeding Quality - A cat is of breeding quality when it exhibits sufficiently superior traits according to the accepted breed standard to be regarded as suitable for participation in the program.

Breed True - When cats of the same breed pass on an identifiable set of physical characteristics from one generation to the next, those traits are said to "breed true." These might include such things as coat color or type, eye color, or physical conformation.

C

Carpal Pads - A cat's carpal pads are found on the animal's front legs at the "wrists." These pads serve to provide additional traction to the animal when walking.

Castrate - Castration is the medical procedure for removing a male cat's testicles to render the animal incapable of reproduction.

Caterwaul - A caterwaul is a high-pitched and strident feline vocalization that is discordant and unpleasant.

Cat Fancy - The "cat fancy" is comprised of those individuals actively interested in breeding, showing, and even simply appreciating cats of various breeds and types as well as the registered associations and clubs to which they belong.

Catnip - Catnip is a perennial herb in the mint family. Its scientific name is Nepeta cataria. Many cats are strongly attracted to catnip and exhibit mild intoxication upon contact with it. However, kittens cannot experience this response until they are at least 6-9 months of age.

Cattery - A cattery is any establishment where cats are housed, usually as part of an organized program of breeding

Certified Pedigree - Certified pedigrees are issued by feline registering associations and are a validated animal's genetic authenticity as a prime example of a given breed.

Clowder - Clowder is a collective name indicating a group of cats gathered in one place at one time.

Coat - Coat is the accepted term used for a cat's fur. The major qualifiers in this regard are long and shorthaired.

Crate - Any small container that can be securely locked and that is used to temporarily confine a cat or other companion animal for the purposes of safe transport is referred to as a "crate."

Crepuscular - Animals exhibiting crepuscular behavior are most active at dawn and dusk, which is the accurate term for the most active periods in a cat's day. It is not correct to say that these animals are nocturnal, even though they possess excellent low light vision.

Crossbred - Any cat that is the product of mating between a dam and a sire of different breeds is crossbred. This may occur as an accident or as an intentional effort to create a new and distinct breed exhibiting desirable qualities of the two foundation breeds.

D

Dam - In a mating pair of cats, the female is often referred to as the "dam."

Dander - Dander refers to the small scales that are shed along with the hair of an animal that is often created by saliva that dried on the fur as a consequence of self-grooming. Dander plays a leading role in the triggering of allergic reactions in people with specific sensitivity. In cats, the protein Fel d 1 in the dander is mainly responsible for this reaction in humans.

Declawing - Declawing is an extremely controversial surgical procedure. The last digit of the cat's toes is removed so that the animal is permanently deprived of its claws. In theory, the procedure developed as an anti-scratching measure, but it is now seen as excessive and cruel and is illegal in Europe and many parts of the United States.

Desex - "Desexing" is an accepted term to describe the procedures, either spaying or neutering, whereby animals are deprived of their ability to reproduce.

Domesticated - Domesticated animals are those creatures that, through long association, have come to be tame and to live in companionship with humans either to work or to serve as companions.

E

Ear Mites - Ear mites are microscopic parasites often present in the ear canals of felines. They cause redness and irritation, leading to an accumulation of black, tarry debris and secondary yeast infections. This is an extremely unpleasant infestation for the cat accompanied by extreme itching. It is detectable not only by the visible inflammation but also by the presence of a strong and unpleasant odor.

Entire - Entire is a term used in the cat fancy to describe an animal that has not been spayed or neutered and has an intact reproductive system.

Exhibitor - An exhibitor is an individual who participates in a cat show either with a cat they own or as a representative of the owner.

F

Fel d 1 - The protein Fel d 1 can be found in cats' sebaceous glands and saliva. It is responsible for causing an allergic reaction in humans who have a specific sensitivity to it. This reaction includes but is not limited to sneezing, watering eyes, nasal congestion, and itching.

Feline - A feline is any animal that is a member of the family Felidae. This group includes "big" cats like lions, tigers, and jaguars, as well as domestic cats.

Fleas - Fleas are parasites of the order Siphonaptera that feed on the host animal's blood they infest. These creatures do not have wings but are well adapted to jump.

Flehmening/Flehmen Reaction - In cats, the Flehmen Reaction is often mistaken as a facial grimace indicating dislike. In reality, this "expression" during which the cat holds its mouth partially open is adopted for the express purpose of allowing air to pass over a special structure in the roof of the mouth just behind the upper front teeth called Jacobsen's Organ. The organ, which is two small holes, functions as a secondary set of nostrils giving the cat the ability to essentially "taste" a scent or odor.

G

Gene pool - The gene pool in any population of organisms refers to the collective genetic information of its diversity and reproduction.

Genes - Genes are the distinct hereditary units responsible for specific characteristics passed down from one generation of organisms to another. Genes consist of a DNA sequence found at a specific location on a chromosome.

Genetic - The term genetics is used about any inherited trait or characteristic identifiable from one generation to the next.

Genetically Linked Defects - Any specific health or physical problem passed from one generation to the next that is, in some way, negative, harmful, or potentially limiting in nature.

Genetics - Genetics is the scientific study of heredity.

Genotype - A genotype refers to the genetic makeup of an organism or a group of organisms.

Groom - Grooming refers to the procedures and protocols involved in caring for the coat of a cat including, but not limited to brushing, combing, trimming, or washing.

Guard Hair - Guard's hairs are longer, coarser hairs that form the outer or top layer of the coat on some breeds of cats.

H

Heat - "Heat" is the commonly accepted term to designate when a female cat reaches the point in seasonal estrus when she is ready to be impregnated by a male.

Hereditary - Hereditary elements, including traits, diseases, or conditions, are genetically transmitted from parents to their offspring.

Histamine - Histamines are physiologically active amines present in plant and animal tissue released from musk cells as part of an allergic reaction.

Hock - In anatomical nomenclature, a hock is that part of a cat's hind leg we would describe as the animal's "ankle."

Housetraining - Housetraining or housebreaking is the process of training a cat to live cleanly in a home with humans utilizing a litter box or pan.

Humane Societies - Humane societies are generally groups working to end animal suffering due to overt cruelty, impoverishment, or similar circumstances. The umbrella organization in the United States is The Humane Society of the United States. In the United Kingdom, it is Humane Society International.

I

Immunization - Immunization is the targeted use of injections for the purpose of cultivating immunity against disease. The injections are also commonly called vaccinations.

Innate - When a quality, tendency, or trait is said to be innate, it has been present since birth.

Inbreeding - The act of inbreeding occurs when two cats with a close filial relationship, like siblings, mate and produce offspring. This results in genetic flaws that become more serious the deeper the inbreeding penetrates into the gene pool.

Instinct - Instincts are innate behavior patterns and come in automatic response to triggering stimuli in the environment.

Intact - Animals with complete reproductive systems are said to be intact because they are still capable of producing offspring.

J

Jacobsen's Organ - In cats, the Jacobsen's Organ is found just behind the upper front teeth on the roof of the mouth. It comprises two small openings that function as second nostrils that allow the cat to "taste" odors or scents.

K

Kindle - Kindle is a collective term that refers to a group of cats in one place at one time. Another word with the same meaning is "clowder."

Kitten - A cat is a kitten when it is less than six months of age.

L

Lactation - Lactation is the physical process by which mammary glands produce and secret milk for the nourishment of young mammals.

Litter - Litter is the collective term for all kittens born at one time to a single mother. Typically this is 3-4, but some litters can be as large as 6-10 or even 12-14 in some breeds.

Litter Box - Litter boxes are really any container of any configuration that is used for the express purpose of providing an indoor cat with a sanitary location to urinate and defecate in a provided collecting material like clay gravel or fine clumping sand.

Longhair - Longhair is a descriptive term for a cat's coat

M

Mites - Small arachnids (Acarina) parasites that infect both animals and plants and are often found in the ear canals of felines.

Moggy - Moggy is a term in the United Kingdom for a mixed breed cat.

Muzzle - A cat's muzzle is part of the head that projects forward and includes the mouth, jaws, and nose. It may alternately be referred to as the snout.

N

Neuter - Neuter is a term that specifically refers to the castration of a male cat to prevent the animal from impregnating females.

Nictitating Membrane - The nictating membrane, or third eyelid, on a cat is an inner transparent eyelid that works to moisten and protect the eye.

Nocturnal- Nocturnal Animals are most active during the night. This term is mistakenly applied to cats. Felines are actually crepuscular, meaning they are most active at dawn and dusk.

O

Odd-Eyed - When a cat is "odd-eyed," it has two eyes of different colors.

P

Papers - A cat's "papers" are the official documentation of the animal's registered pedigree verifying the authenticity of its lineage as part of a designated breed.

Pedigree - A pedigree is essentially a cat's family tree or genealogy set in writing and covering three or more generations. The record is used to clearly establish the animal's genetic authenticity within a specific breed.

Pet Quality - Purebred cats that are designated to be "pet quality" have some physical characteristics or characteristics that diverge sufficiently from the accepted standard for the breed that they are not considered candidates to be shown or to be used in a breeding program.

Q

Queen - A female cat with an intact reproductive system is called a queen.

Quick - The quick of a cat's claw is the vascular "pink" just behind the white nail that will bleed profusely if it is accidentally clipped.

R

Rabies - Rabies is a highly infectious viral disease typically fatal to warm-blooded animals. It is transmitted by a bite from an infected individual and attacks the central nervous system causing severely aggressive behavior.

Registered Name - The cat's registered name is the registered agent's official name on the animal's pedigree. The name is typically long and contains multiple references to the ancestry of the individual.

S

Scratching Post - A scratching "post" is any structure covered in carpet, rope, or similar material that has been constructed for the express purpose of allowing a domestic cat to sharpen and clean its claws without being destructive to household furnishings.

Shelter - A shelter is any local or regional organization that works to rescue and care for stray, homeless animals with the end goal of placing them in permanent homes.

Show Quality - Show quality cats are individuals that meet the official breed standard for their type and are thus recognized as suitable to be exhibited in cat shows and to be used in breeding programs

Sire - In a breeding pair of cats, the sire is the male member.

Spay - Spaying is the procedure whereby the ovaries of a female cat are removed to render the animal incapable of producing offspring.

Spraying - Spraying is territorial behavior most typically present in male cats involving a stream of pungent urine emissions to serve as a territorial marker.

Stud - Studs are male cats with intact testicles so that they are suitable to serve as half of a mating pair in a breeding program.

T

Tapetum Lucidum - The tapetum lucidum is the interior portion of the feline eye that is highly reflective and aids in night vision. This is the portion of the eye that glows in photographs taken with a flash.

V

Vaccine - A vaccine is a preparation of a weakened or dead pathogen like a bacterium or virus. The vaccine is used to stimulate antibody production to create immunity against disease.

W

Wean - Weaning is the point at which a mother cat breaks her kittens away from subsisting on the milk she produces so that they begin to draw their primary nutrition from solid food.

Whisker Pad - The whisker pad is the thickened area on either side of a cat's face where the animal's sensory whiskers are anchored.

Whole - A whole cat is an individual of either gender with a functioning reproductive system.

Useful Contacts

If you own a cat, this is one list you should keep near you. In an emergency when you need help with your feline friend the following contacts should come in handy.

USA

Animal Legal Defense Fund: (707) 795-2533

Do you suspect that one of your neighbors is abusing their pet? Are you having problems with your landlord or tenants because you have a companion animal? Do you want to report a veterinarian who you suspect is acting unethically or illegally? Here is the phone number to dial. The Animal Legal Defense Fund can assist with landlord-tenant issues, veterinarian issues, neglect, and abuse of any kind. The Animal Legal Defense Fund's mission is to use the legal system to protect the lives and interests of animals. ALDF achieves this mission by filing high-impact lawsuits to protect animals from harm, providing free legal assistance and training to prosecutors to ensure that animal abusers are held accountable for their crimes, supporting tough animal protection legislation and opposing harmful animal protection legislation, and providing resources and opportunities to law students and professionals to advance the emerging field of animal law.

ASPCA (aspca.org)

The American Society for the Prevention of Cruelty to Animals.

AVMA (avma.org)

The AVMA website contains a lot of helpful information, including first aid procedures for bleeding, burns, heatstroke, choking, fractures, shock, lack of breathing, and lack of a heartbeat. Although much of the site is designed for veterinarians, it also contains sections for the public.

Emergency Disaster Information Line: 1 800 227 4645

This number, provided by the American Humane Association, provides support and relief information for pet owners living in areas affected by disasters such as earthquakes, hurricanes, flooding, and fire, among others. While this is not an official "hotline," it is operated by live people who can direct pet owners in the event of a natural disaster or emergency.

Pet Poison Helpline: 855-764-7661

Every second counts in an emergency. Is it possible that your cat ate something poisonous? Call your veterinarian or the Pet Poison Helpline right away. The sooner you diagnose cat poisoning, the easier, less expensive, and safer it is to treat your pet. Pet Poison Helpline is a 24-hour animal poison control service for pet owners and veterinary professionals in the United States, Canada, and the Caribbean. They need help treating a potentially poisoned pet. They are available 24 hours a day, seven days a week, to assist any poisoned pet with any type of poisoning. There is a $49 fee for this service, which could potentially save your cat's life.

Pet Travel Hotline: 1800 545 USDA

If you intend to travel by plane with your cat, a quick call to this number will ensure that you are prepared for any bumps in the road involving your cat. The Animal and Plant Health Inspection Service of the United States Department of Agriculture operates this hotline, which provides travel resources, licensed pet transporter contact information, rules and regulations, and assistance to those who believe their animal was treated inhumanely travel.

Spay/Neuter Helpline: 1 800 248 SPAY

Every year, thousands of cats are abandoned or euthanized as a result of irresponsible breeding. The North Shore Animal League is a non-profit organization that works to America's SpayUSA is a nationwide network and referral service for low-cost spay/neuter procedures. SpayUSA, founded in 1993, has assisted hundreds of thousands of people nationwide in obtaining low-cost, high-quality spay/neuter services for over 20 years. The SpayUSA referral service can help anyone who needs help finding affordable spay/neuter services.

UK

GCCF (gccfcats.org)

the UK's premier cat registration body. The GCCF offers information, advice and expertise to help choose, care for, or breed the right cat for you or to show.

Muffin & Poppy (muffinandpoppy.co.uk)

The UK's #1 British Shorthair lovers and breeders. In the Muffin & Poppy's website you will find useful resources and information about the gorgeous British Shorthair cats.

RSPCA (rspca.org.uk)

The Royal Society for the Prevention of Cruelty to Animals is a charity operating in England and Wales that promotes animal welfare.

TICA (tica.org)

The International Cat Association (TICA), the world's largest genetic registry of pedigreed and domestic cats.

NOTE: In addition to these national helpline and hotline numbers, keep the phone numbers for your local vet, nearest emergency vet, and local animal control services on hand.

About The Author

Eric De Souza has lived with cats for most of his life and is particular fond of the gorgeous and ever so popular British Shorthair. He has studied feline psychology and have been breeding British Shorthairs for over a decade.

Made in the USA
Monee, IL
26 November 2023

47399135R00094